Cleopatra

to

Christ

Cleopatra
to
Christ

Jesus was the great grandson of Cleopatra VII.

by
Ralph Ellis

Edfu Books

Adventures Unlimited

Cleopatra to Christ

First published in 2006 by Edfu Books

Published in the U.K. by:
Edfu Books
PO Box 165
Cheshire
CW8 4WF
info@edfu-books.com
U.K.

Published in the U.S.A. by:
Adventures Unlimited
PO Box 74
Kempton, Illinois
60946
auphq@frontier.net
U.S.A.

First edition July 2006

U.K. paperback edition
ISBN 0-9531913-3-8 (978-0-9531913-3-8)

U.S.A. paperback edition
ISBN 1-931882-64-9

Printed in the United Kingdom by T.J. International, Padstow.

The moon herself grew dark, rising at sunset,
Covering her suffering in the night,
Because she saw her beautiful namesake, Selene,
Breathless, descending to Hades,
With her she had had the beauty of her light in common,
And mingled her own darkness with her death.

Eulogy to Cleopatra Selene.

Ourania, o'er her star-bespangled lyre,
With touch of majesty diffused her soul;
A thousand tones, that in the breast inspire,
Exalted feelings, o 'er the wires 'gan roll—
She sang of night that clothed the infant world,
In strains as solemn as its dark profound—
How at the call of Jove the mist unfurled,
And o'er the swelling vault—the glowing sky,
The newborn stars hung out their lamps on high,
And rolled their mighty orbs to music's sweetest sound.

Ode to Muse Ourania,
James Percival.

First and foremost I would like to dedicate this book to Mr A J Bethell, who researched and ruminated on this same topic nearly 100 years ago and deposited his resulting manuscript in the British Library. It is my belief that Mr Bethell missed much of the available evidence and arrived at the wrong conclusions; however, the manuscript he created was certainly the inspiration upon which this book was founded.

Secondly, I would like to thank Mike Dash, who wrote a letter to the Daily Mail listing the many bizarre book titles he had found. Among these titles was the manuscript by Mr Bethell, which is how I discovered it. In Mike Dash's defence, it has to be admitted that Mr Bethell's argument, that Jesus was the son of Queen Cleopatra, stretched both chronology and biology to its very limits. However, Mr Bethell had also highlighted a number of key points that allowed me to discover the real truth about the ancestry of Jesus. My thanks to both of you.

Finally I would like to thank Margaret, my travelling companion on my tour of Jordan, whose knowledge of history and the classics was inspirational and made the trip memorable. If I can be as youthful at the age of 83, I will consider myself very lucky.

Ralph Ellis
November 2006
Cheshire.

www.edfu-books.com

Contents

Intro

Royal Family

In my previous works, I have demonstrated that Jesus was a prince, related in some manner to the Egyptian royal line. But the finer details of exactly who Jesus was related to, and how far back into Egyptian history one needed to go in order to find these family links, were unclear. The problem being, of course, that any potential researcher of the New Testament story has very little to go on. The biblical and historical accounts that detail Jesus' birth and ancestry can be summarised in a single paragraph, and that is simply not enough information to place him into the historical record – or is it?

This children's story of the life of Jesus, as it is presented to us in the New Testament accounts, is well known. He was supposedly a poor carpenter born in a stable, a disadvantaged child who rose to become a great leader and teacher. However, as I demonstrated in the book *Jesus,* this fairy-tale bears no resemblance to the truth whatsoever. There is more than enough evidence within the biblical texts themselves to conclusively prove that Jesus' family were actually wealthy, educated and influential characters within Judaean society.

Jesus himself was not a carpenter but a *tekton* or an 'architect'; although this term probably refers more to the speculative side of the masonic Craft than the construction profession. He received a good education in Egypt, at a time when the majority of the population were illiterate. His friends, Zacharias and Nicodemus, were very rich; while another supporter, Joanna, was the wife of Herod's vizier or prime minister. It was also demonstrated in the book *Jesus,* by carefully scrutinising the accounts of Josephus Flavius, that Jesus was governor of Tiberias, owned a castle in that region and controlled a private militia some 600 strong. More importantly, Jesus' birth was deemed by Herod to be a threat to his royal lineage, forcing him to apparently kill all the male infants in the region in order to eradicate this pretender to the throne – an act or rumour which clearly demonstrates that Jesus was a prince of some influence within Judaean society. In fact, the mocking claim of Jesus to be the 'King of the Jews' was no mockery at all, for he was indeed a legitimate pretender to many of the thrones of the Middle East. Undoubtedly, Jesus' parents' ultimate goal was to see him seated upon one of those thrones, which is why the king and tetrarchs of Judaea feared his presence in that region.

I have also previously demonstrated the strong links between Jesus and Egypt, which is why my first book on this topic was entitled *Jesus, Last of the Pharaohs*. However, at that point in time I was unable to discover in what way Jesus could have been related to the Egyptian royal line. Unfortunately, the texts of the Bible and Talmud are incomplete and both show obvious signs of heavy editing. If Jesus was truly a pretender to the thrones of the Near East, a legitimate royal pretender of Egyptian heritage, it was in nobody's interest to further his claims by recording his true ancestry. So the biblical texts have left us with vague commentaries on his parents and siblings, and two biblical genealogies in the New Testament that completely contradict each other.

The additional paragraphs that refer to Jesus in the works of Josephus Flavius, which I have highlighted in previous works, add a great deal more information about the former's life. They again demonstrate Jesus' wealth and status, but they add precious little to his family background and ancestry. One paragraph in each of Josephus' *Antiquities* and *The Jewish War* calls Jesus the 'Egyptian False Prophet', which again demonstrates the possible links with the pharaonic dynasties, but does little to explain his parentage.

However, if my assertion is true and Jesus was descended from the Egyptian royal line, then a number of problems arise which some of my more vociferous detractors have described as being 'insurmountable'. Firstly, if Jesus was of the royal line of Egypt, what was he doing in Judaea? Secondly, if Jesus was of the royal line of Egypt, why was his birth visited by Magi from Persia, instead of *sem*-priests from Egypt? Thirdly, if Jesus was of the royal line of Egypt, his presence in Judaea implied that he had been exiled from his former homeland. For what reason and at what time was such an illustrious family exiled to Judaea?

Egyptian or Persian?

The problem is this. The various texts that detail the circumstances of Jesus' birth and education would seem to be incompatible. According to these, we would appear to be looking into the historical record for an exiled prince who was of both Egyptian and Persian descent. In addition, we need to discover a prince who was influential enough to make his mark on the history of Judaea, but obscure enough to be easily lost to most of real recorded history. The question is, therefore, whether any prince within the historical record would fit all of these widely differing requirements.

Strange as it may seem, there is such a royal family. They were indeed influential kings and queens, and yet it is known that they were exiled from their homeland and settled in an area called Bethanya [Bethany], near Judaea, in about AD 4. They brought with them into exile 500 cavalry and 100 relations and retinue; an account which tallies with Josephus' accounts of the biblical family maintaining their own military forces. In Syrio-Judaea, this exiled royal family raised a new generation and founded a new society that competed strongly with the traditional Judaean authorities in Jerusalem.

Moreover, members of this exiled royal family were not only directly related to Queen Cleopatra VII of Egypt, but also to Emperor Julius Caesar of Rome and to King Phraates IV of Parthia (or Persia). In other words, this family was hugely influential, relatively unknown, suddenly impoverished and, in addition, uniquely related to all three of the major empires of this era. With its enfeebled exiled circumstances this family was essentially powerless, but never without influence. They were also impoverished, for a royal family with such an illustrious pedigree, but never without wealthy, well-placed backers and supporters.

Here, we have a previously influential royal family living in obscure exile in biblical Bethany, and yet this is a family that appears to meet all of our diverse requirements. This was indeed a family that would have been visited by the Parthian Magi, yet is likely to have educated its sons in Egypt. This was indeed a family that could have made Herod (the tetrarch) fear for his position, sufficient for him to want to eliminate all the male children of Judaea.

The sparse historical facts that detail the life of this royal family seem to fit our list of requirements rather well, but the unanswered question is: was this really the family of the biblical Jesus and his brothers and sisters? As this story unfolds, readers will find a wealth of compelling circumstantial evidence that leads us towards an earth-shattering conclusion – that Jesus was directly descended from Julius Caesar of Rome, Queen Cleopatra VII of Egypt and King Phraates IV of Parthia. But in the end, despite all of the evidence, only the reader can decide if the case has been proven.

Notes to the reader

a. Because of the radical nature of this book, it has been necessary to highlight the difference between standard orthodox assumptions and those generated by my lateral view of theology. Throughout this book, therefore, I have used curved brackets ( ) to denote orthodox assumptions and square brackets [ ] to denote my radical new assumptions. I hope that this serves to clarify the text.

b. The references in the text are numerous. To ease the problem of continuously referring to the reference section at the back of the book, some references have been prefixed. Prefixes are as follows:

B = Bible, K = Koran, J = Josephus, T = Talmud, S = Strabo
M = Manetho, N = Nag Hammadi, KN = Kebra Nagast.

It may also be advantageous to explain in modern terms some of the locations that are being discussed.

Armenia	=	Kurdish region in eastern Turkey and western Iraq.
Auranitis	=	region to the east of the river Jordan.
Aurania	=	see Auranitis above.
Babylon	=	southern and eastern Iraq.
Bactria	=	east of the Caspian Sea. Afghanistan and Turkmenistan.
Bithynia	=	northeastern Turkey.
Bethanya	=	region to the east of the river Jordan.
Cappadocia	=	southeastern Turkey.
Hadramaut	=	Yemen.
Gaulanitis	=	the Golan Heights northeast of the Sea of Galilee.
Israel	=	region to the west of the Sea of Galilee.
Judaea	=	region around Jerusalem.
Lydia	=	western Turkey, near the Maeander river.
Mauretania	=	central and western North Africa.
Media	=	northwestern Iran.
Najd	=	Saudi Arabia.
Parthia	=	originally Bactria, but the empire spread to Iran, Iraq and eastern Turkey.
Persia	=	an earlier empire occupying roughly the same region as Parthia.
Samaria	=	region to the west of the river Jordan.
Scythia	=	Ukraine. Sometimes given as Bactria.
Syria	=	Modern Syria, but sometimes a term for all of the Levantine coast including Judaea, Israel and Tyre.

I

Chess Game

The entire foundation for this new history of the New Testament lies upon the historical fact that a powerful, but relatively obscure, royal family was exiled from Parthia (Persia) in about AD 4. They travelled with their courtiers, relatives and a small army to Syria, which at that time came under the control of the Herod tetrarchs (three of the sons of Herod the Great). There, they built a new city state that declared its independence from Jerusalem and Damascus, and it is entirely possible that one of their sons eventually declared himself as 'king' of the region. The argument I shall be pursuing, which is admittedly speculative at this moment in time, is that this governor of an insignificant city state in Syrio-Judaea was the biblical Jesus.

But if this character was so insignificant, then why did he and his family cause such ripples in the geopolitics of the Near East during the first century AD? The answer lies in his ancestry because, as I have already suggested, he was related to all of the key players in that era's royal and political chess game. The evidence for this will grow as the chapters progress, but perhaps we should digress for a while to look at the chess board itself, and the various pieces that were upon it in this era.

Egypt

Egypt had been under the control of the Persians twice between 525 and 332 BC, but after Alexander the Great's defeat of Darius III at Issus in southeastern Turkey, Egypt came under the control of the Macedonian Greeks. Alexander died in 323 BC and, after a few power struggles, Egypt came under the control of the Ptolemaic dynasty, who were descendants of Alexander's general Ptolemy, son of Lagus. Egypt remained powerful under the Ptolemaic pharaohs, with many of the fine temples we see today in Upper Egypt being completed during this era. She was also a key player in the politics of the wider regions, but the nation's undoing was the constant sibling rivalry for the throne.

Time after time the Ptolemaic kings and queens of Egypt were ruthlessly deposed, and this instability drained the nation's resources. This problem became a crisis when Ptolemy Aulets XII, the flute player, was exiled to Rome during a general uprising. In Rome, Ptolemy XII plotted his return to Egypt and was eventually successful in 55 BC, but crucially this was achieved with Roman assistance and might. This backing of Rome signalled the end of Egypt as an independent nation and thus we find that Ptolemy XII's famous daughter, Cleopatra VII, essentially became a vassal of Rome. Cleopatra did attempt, as we shall see, to turn the political and strategic tables on the Romans, but all her plotting and scheming eventually came to nothing and Egypt was to remain a conquered nation.

Rome

One of many legends has it that Rome was founded by Prince Aeneas, who fled from the ruins of the sacked city of Troy. This mythology is interesting, given the alternative location for the city of Troy that I suggested in the book *Eden*. However, the Roman Republic was not founded until much later, in 509 BC according to Livy. Having grown steadily in power, the Romans flexed their might against Greece in the early third century BC and the Phoenicians of Carthage in the late third century BC. The republic then grew in size and influence to become masters of the Mediterranean and beyond. This potted history takes us up to the era of Julius Caesar and his close association with Cleopatra VII of Egypt; a topic which will be addressed in more detail later.

Parthia

The Parthians originated in the Iranian highlands, to the west of the Caspian Sea. They were consummate horsemen, and their mounted archers played a key role in establishing the resulting Arsacid dynasty. This association with mounted archers is an important element in this story, as this elite force became a prime symbol on Parthian coinage and it therefore identifies a key biblical player as being of Parthian origin.

Around 250 BC King Arsaces, after whom the dynasty is named, took his forces out of modern Turkmenistan and rode deep into Seleucid (Persian) territory. Having taken the city of Herat, a prime city on the major trade route known as the Silk Road, the Hellenistic Seleucid empire of Persia that had been founded by Alexander the Great collapsed, and the Arsacid empire of the Parthians took control. The borders of this new empire were pushed out westwards until they impinged upon the eastern borders of the expanding Roman Empire, and the boundary between the two lay in or around the eastern borders of modern Syria.

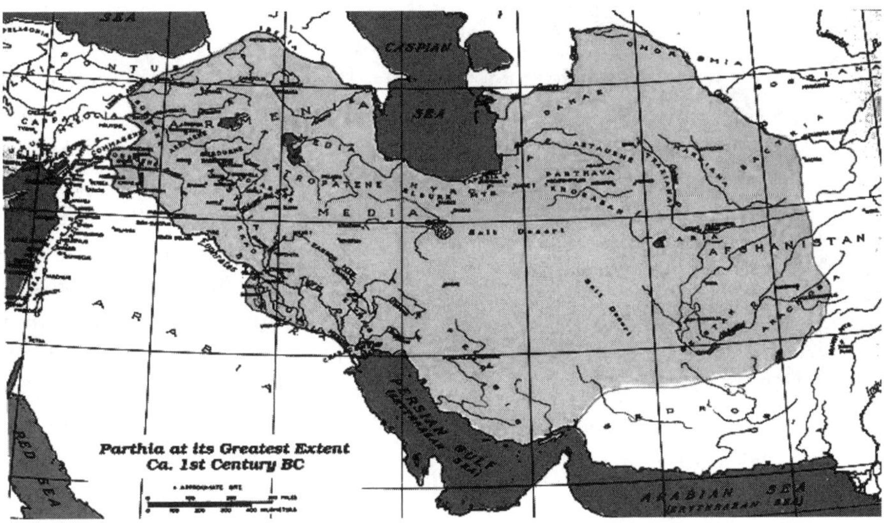

Fig 1. The Parthian Empire in the first century BC.

Judaea

Sandwiched between these three key players, who were each vying for the territories of the Near East, was the insignificant but key nation of Judaeo-Israel. The population of Judaeo-Israel was a fusion of many (often related) nationalities, including Jews, Canaanites, Phoenicians, Judaeo-Persians, and Syrians. However, Strabo says that the majority of the citizens of Judaea were Egyptians, and this observation equates well with my proposals that the Jews not only came from Egypt (upon the biblical exodus) but were actually Egyptians themselves.

Judaeo-Israel was essentially a Roman vassal state, which was

Fig 2. The Treasury, one of the Nabatean 'tombs' at Petra.

governed by King Herod the Great from 37 to 4 BC. Although Herod was a vassal of Rome and was required to do their bidding, Cleopatra VII was becoming very influential in Roman politics and so Herod had to contend with Cleopatra's fickle whims and policies too.

Cleopatra's primary desire was to enlarge her kingdom and influence, and she was quite happy to manipulate her 'husband' Mark Antony to achieve her ends. Cleopatra had already persuaded Antony to give her Phoenicia, some of the Arabias and the southern portion of Judaea around Jericho, after his successful campaigns in the region in 34 BC, but there was still the troublesome semi-independent province of Judaeo-Israel that lay at the outer reaches of her growing empire.

Accordingly, Cleopatra encouraged Antony to get Herod to attack King Malchus of Nabataea (Petra), indicating that this was to punish Nabataea for late payment of its tribute to Egypt. However, this demand came at a highly inopportune moment for Herod, as Mark Antony had just entered into a civil war with Octavian-Augustus Caesar and could have benefited from the support that Herod had promised him. Herod dutifully attacked Nabataea, but then Cleopatra undermined the whole campaign by supporting the Nabataeans! There was a logic in this madness, even if the logic was highly skewed with duplicity, treachery and avarice. As Josephus recalls:

> And now Cleopatra persuaded Antony to entrust Herod (the Great) with the war against the Arabs – if he won she would become mistress of Arabia, if he lost, the mistress of Judaea. She would be using one ruler to get rid of the other. [J1]

In other words, Cleopatra was manipulating all and sundry, including her 'husband' Mark Antony, in order to further her goal of Egyptian world domination. King Herod the Great was thus placed in a very awkward and dangerous position, and there was a great danger that he would eventually be deposed by his stronger Egyptian 'ally'. However, fortune was smiling on Herod in his moment of adversity, as it had so many times before.

Herod was a loyal supporter of Mark Antony, but at Cleopatra's insistence he had been in Arabia during the great sea-battle of Actium. Mark Antony was comprehensively defeated by Octavian-Augustus in this sea-battle so Herod had lost his powerful Roman mentor and ally, and now Augustus Caesar ruled all of the Roman empire. Crucially, however, Herod's absence from the battle of Actium meant that he had not actually fought against Augustus, and so he was able to beg the forgiveness of the new emperor and retain his Judaean kingship.

That Herod managed to juggle these many competing rivalries in the international political arena, plus his many internal problems, shows that he was in many ways a consummate diplomat and an astute ruler – before age and jealousy befuddled his senses. Herod died in 4 BC and since he could not decide on a successor, the kingdom was bequeathed to three of his sons; Herod Archelous gained control of Judaea, Herod Antipas of Israel and Herod Philip of Syria. It is Herod Philip who becomes central to the unfolding story, as it is in the Syrian provinces that the exiled royal family from Parthia settled.

To the east of Judaea and to the south of Syria lay the relatively insignificant nation of Nabataea, which Herod had been preoccupied with, whose capital city was the famed yet concealed city of Petra. The Nabataeans were a Semitic people who may have been related to the Sabeans of Yemen, and spoke an Aramaic (Hebrew) dialect. The Nabataeans were not major players in this epic drama, but they were said to have assisted the exiled Parthian royalty in the construction of their new city in southern Syria.

Biblical Judaea

In addition to this secular history of Judaea, we also have the accounts of the New Testament. Here we discover another problem, for when dealing with the biblical accounts we enter a completely new world; and this is not one bedeviled by the usual historical uncertainty, but instead it is bedeviled by the scourge of deliberate deception. Saul (St Paul), the creator of Christianity, and the Christian clergy who followed him, never needed a historical foundation for their iconic hero, Jesus. In fact, many details of his true ancestry are likely to have clashed spectacularly with the new ideology that the Church leaders were trying to peddle. By necessity, therefore, all mention of Jesus' family history was censored from the outset. Saul only needed an icon to sell to the plebeians, and this was an icon that was fully divorced from its historical reality. In fact, the reputation of the early Church was such that the letters of Peter had to plead with congregations that there had been no fabrications or adulterations of the text:

> For we have not followed cunningly devised fables, when we made known unto you the power and coming of our Lord Jesus Christ, but were eyewitnesses of his majesty. [B2]

But the truth was that much of the New Testament had been altered and amended during the first few centuries of Christian history. While Saul may well have initiated these distortions to true history, one of the prime suspects for the later amendments to the original text has to be Bishop Eusebius, who has been described as:

> ...the first thoroughly dishonest and unfair historian of ancient times. [3]

One of the first casualties of this editing and censorship was Jesus' marriage to Mary Magdalene. The fact that Jesus was married has received a major boost recently with the publication of *The Da Vinci Code*; however, many books have previously championed this otherwise unmentionable fact, including my own *Jesus, Last of the Pharaohs*. The Church has softened its stance in recent years and the abject denials of Jesus' marriage have now evolved into the occasional response of 'there is no evidence' or even 'it is always possible'. However, the truth is that the Bible itself describes the marriage of Jesus and Mary Magdalene in the verses that discuss the marriage at Cana, as I pointed out in the book *Jesus*. The Book of Revelations makes this even clearer when it says:

> Let us be glad and rejoice, and give honour to him: for the marriage of the Lamb is come, and his wife hath made herself ready. And to her was granted that she should be arrayed in fine linen, clean and white: for the fine linen is the righteousness of saints. And he saith unto me, Write, Blessed are they which are called unto the marriage supper of the Lamb. [B4]

> And there came unto me one of the seven angels which had the seven vials full of the seven last plagues, and talked with me, saying, Come hither, I will show thee the bride, the Lamb's wife. [B5]

The Lamb is, of course a reference to Jesus himself. The Catholic Church tries vainly to persuade us that the 'wife' in these verses actually pertains to the Church itself – that Jesus was being accepted into a 'marriage' to the Church. But it is obvious to anyone who is in full command of their faculties that the 'wife' was the true physical wife of Jesus – Mary Magdalene.

Not only has this marriage of Jesus been divorced *(sic)* from its true historical reality, but so too has the wider biblical narrative. We have all heard the stories from the New Testament in which Jesus did this, the disciples did that, and the Romans were doing something in the background. But what these stories never attempt to do is place these biblical events into the wider perspective of the geopolitics of first millennium Judaeo-Israel. As we have already seen, contrary to the biblical perception of history, Judaea was not the main focus of attention in this era; instead, it was simply a minute element within a much larger political picture, a minnow in a pool of giant predators that swarmed around it. Judaea only came through many of these political upheavals relatively unscathed because it was a convenient buffer region to the wider strategic manoeuvres and battles that were going on all around it. Mark Antony had already received a bloody nose in his clashes with the Parthian army, so as long as Judaea maintained good relations with Rome it could happily act as a mercenary army for the Empire. Had Judaeo-Israel been a little more diplomatic in its later internal struggles and its dispute with Rome, it would doubtless have escaped its eventual destruction in AD 70.

The New Testament and the Christian clergy try their utmost to convince us that Jesus was a political and social nobody in this political maelstrom between Parthia and Rome, and so they attempt to convince their followers that Jesus was a humble carpenter, who happened to change the theology of an entire region. So is it possible that the Church authorities are correct, and Jesus was simply the political nonentity of popular mythology? Is this the reason that he does not seem to appear in any of the historical accounts of the Near East?

The fairy stories that emanate from the Church would like us to think so, but if Jesus and the actions that he took were in any way important to the wider world in this era, it is much more likely that this was because he belonged to or was related to that larger political picture in some manner. The way in which he was a part of that wider perspective is the primary subject of this book, for as I have already stated, it is highly likely that he was a direct descendant of Queen Cleopatra VII of Egypt and King Phraates IV of Parthia. It was only because his royal ancestry was known to the authorities in this era that anyone took any notice of him in the first place, and it was again this royal heritage that allowed him to speak his mind without getting into too much trouble. For Jesus had friends in high places, as the Bible readily admits. The Babylonian Talmud, the Jewish commentary on the Old Testament, says exactly the same thing when it relates:

> Rabbi Papa said 'This is (Mary Magdalene) of which they say, "She was the descendant of princes and rulers, she played the harlot with carpenters." ' [T6]

In other words, the Judaic priesthood understood that Mary Magdalene was a royal princess; so is this what the authors of the New Testament were trying so valiantly to hide from us? But why would the Christian Church prefer its heroes to be paupers, rather than influential royals? What was the political situation in the years leading up to the birth of Jesus, and why was this royal heritage so contentious that the Catholic Church initiated a cover-up that has lasted for over two millennia?

As is usual in any era, there was a web of allegiances and disputes between the leading players in world politics at this time. As we have seen, the three leading contenders for power in the Western and Eastern Empires in the first century before the birth of Jesus were: Egypt, under the rule of Cleopatra VII; Rome, which was just stabilising itself under the autocratic rule of Julius Caesar; and Parthia (Persia), which was ruled by Phraates IV of the Arsacid dynasty. Between them, these rulers held sway over most of Europe, the Middle East and North Africa. There were some disputes and wars between these empires, but there was cooperation too. The following is a potted history of the primary players in this international chess game.

Julius Caesar

Julius, who was born in 100 BC, had conquered Gaul (France) in the 50s BC and wanted to return to Rome in triumph. The Senate, ever fearful of the might of the Roman army, ordered Julius to disband his army and return alone. Julius ignored the Senate and crossed the Rubicon, the frontier of Rome, with one of his legions in 49 BC. By law, Roman armies were not allowed into Rome and so this deliberate act of insubordination ignited a civil war. The Senate rallied around Julius Caesar's former partner in the First Triumvirate, Pompeius Magnus, who is more commonly called Pompey. But Julius Caesar proved the more able army commander, and having pursued Pompey's armies around Spain and Italy, Julius Caesar finally defeated Pompey at the battle of Pharsalus in Greece in 48 BC. Pompey escaped the battle scene and fled to Egypt, but was killed on his arrival there. It was in Egypt that Julius Caesar, having pursued Pompey to these shores, was to meet Cleopatra VII.

I *Chess Game*

Cleopatra

The history and legends of Cleopatra VII, the most famous of all the Cleopatra queens of Egypt, intertwine and mingle so that the one cannot be separated from the other. Here was a glamorous, intelligent and successful queen, a woman who was not shy of using her womanly charms to fulfil her personal advancement and Egypt's political strategy. The spectacle and pomp of her reign were truly awe-inspiring, with the queen boasting that she could spend ten million *sesterces* on a single meal.* In a similar fashion, Shakespeare says of Cleopatra's mighty flagship at the start of the famous battle of Actium:

> The barge she sat in, like a burnished throne,
> Burned on the water; the poop was beaten gold,
> Purple the sails, and so perfumed, that
> The winds were love-sick with them,
> the oars were silver. [7]

Purple was, of course, the inordinately expensive dye controlled by the Phoenicians in Tyre. So expensive was it, and so vivid the hue, that it became the colour of kings and emperors. It is said that the imagery of Cecil B de Mille's or Joseph Mankiewicz's epic films about Cleopatra adversely colour our perceptions, but perhaps they were not so far wide of the mark in their lavish portrayals. This was truly an age when royal spectacle confirmed royal authority and cowed the rebellious masses. As long as the workers had their bread and beer, who would be so bold as to deny that Cleopatra was a daughter of the gods?

Cleopatra VII was born in 69 BC, the daughter of the Greco-Egyptian Pharaoh Ptolemy XII. After a short co-regency with her father, who died in 51 BC, Cleopatra married her younger brother Ptolemy XIII. Relations between brother and sister were obviously strained, as an armed dispute ensued during which Cleopatra was forced to flee to Judaea or Syria in the spring of 48 BC. Ever resourceful, however, Cleopatra gathered an army together and re-invaded Egypt from the east, but the battle was inconclusive.

It was at this very moment that Pompey turned up in Egypt, hotly pursued by Julius Caesar. Ptolemy XIII, Cleopatra's brother, thought he

* Since a slave could cost 6,000 *sesterces*, one might speculate that one *sesterce* had the equivalent value of a modern Euro. Cleopatra is reputed to have achieved her claim by dissolving a large pearl earring in vinegar and drinking it.

would ingratiate himself with Julius by murdering Pompey and presenting the new Roman emperor with his enemy's severed head. However, the cunning plan spectacularly backfired, as Julius Caesar was still an admirer of Pompey, despite their mutual hostilities. In addition, Ptolemy had actually been a supporter of Pompey before his defeat, and so Ptolemy's cowardly treachery earned himself the displeasure of Julius Caesar and a place in Dante's *Inferno* as an arch-traitor.

The previous pharaoh of Egypt, Ptolemy XII, had decreed that Rome should arbitrate if there was a dispute between his children, and so Julius Caesar proceeded to do so. Ptolemy XIII tried to prevent this mediation by blocking Cleopatra's attempts to visit Julius, and this is why legends say that she was delivered to him in a carpet roll (in a pile of bedclothes according to Plutarch). [8]

Whether or not Julius was infatuated with Cleopatra at this point in time, he did try to arbitrate fairly. But a civil war broke out in Alexandria and Julius Caesar had to temporarily flee for his life. However, in the ensuing melee, Ptolemy XIII drowned in the Nile and his other sister Arsinoe was arrested. When all the dust settled in the spring of 47 BC, Cleopatra VII was sole ruler of Egypt and was enjoying a Nile cruise as the lover of Julius Caesar. Egypt was not short of wealth or resources, but it desperately lacked a formidable army. However, a union, both political and personal, between Egypt and Rome would surely produce the empire to end all empires. Cleopatra's strategic aims and dreams were all approaching fruition in the ecstasy of sexual union.

Fig 3. Bust of Cleopatra VII.

It would be nice to leave the story at this blissful moment, with the great Sun-god Ra setting on the western horizon and the two imperial lovers entwined in each others' arms, enjoying a vintage red from crystal glasses. But, unfortunately for them, the politics of this era were not that stable. Julius Caesar was assassinated in 44 BC and Cleopatra, who had been in Rome at the time, fled back to Egypt with her son Caesarion. The Roman empire was then split up into the Second Triumvirate, with Mark Antony in the Near East, Octavian (Augustus) in Rome and Lepidus in Spain.

Marcus Antonius, or Mark Antony, had been a leading supporter of Julius Caesar and after his assassination, Antony was given control over Rome's eastern regions. Part of Antony's plan for control of the Near East was a strategic alliance with Cleopatra of Egypt. Likewise, Cleopatra saw in Antony another potential leader of all the Roman empire, and so she consummated a strategic and personal alliance with Mark Antony in 41 BC. This dual union was to bear fruit with twins, Alexander Helios and Cleopatra Selene in 40 BC. Despite his youthful age, the boy twin, Alexander, was given nominal rule over all of Parthia and the east, even though these kingdoms had not yet been conquered by this new Romo-Egyptian alliance. One cannot help seeing Cleopatra's influence here – it was not necessarily Antony who wanted to conquer and rule Parthia (Persia), but Cleopatra. Parthia was the old mortal enemy of Egypt, not Rome, and the newly crowned prince Alexander Helios bore the dynastic titles of Egypt, not of Rome.

Phraates

Parthia (Persia) does not really enter this tangled tale until a few years after Julius Caesar's death. It is thought that King Phraates IV was born in about 60 BC, and he came to the throne in 37 BC. But there is a problem with Parthian history, and that is that there is very little of it, for some reason:

> They left few records; indeed, we really know very little of the internal history of the Parthians, and would have known still less but for the frequent wars between them and the Greeks and Romans. [9]

This dearth of information makes us overly reliant not only on Roman records, as the quote indicates, but also on the Judaean historian Josephus Flavius. King Herod of Judaea tried not to tangle with the powerful Parthians, but the two nations were close neighbours and so the politics of Parthia were mentioned in the works of Josephus on more than one occasion.

As has already been mentioned, the triumvir of Rome in this region was Mark Antony, who had concluded a strategic and personal alliance with Cleopatra VII of Egypt. With Egyptian support and funding, Antony attacked Phraates IV in Parthia almost immediately after he had come to the throne. But Antony's war against Parthia went badly, and he was forced to withdraw with heavy losses. Even worse, the Roman Triumvirate alliance fell apart and Antony found himself at war with Octavian (Augustus) in Rome. Antony was forced to cede much of his territory in the far east in order to shore up his position on his western borders with Octavian.

This western pressure on Antony's forces should have made Phraates' kingdom relatively safe, but an internal dispute threw up a pretender to the throne called Tiridates, who managed to depose Phraates IV in about 32 BC. But Phraates counter attacked a few years later, and Tiridates fled to the Romans.

Rome was not faring much better, as far as internal stability was concerned, and Mark Antony was eventually defeated at the great sea-battle of Actium in 31 BC. Antony returned to Egypt, defeated and despairing. The dreams of both Antony and Cleopatra had evaporated, and both were reputed to have died at their own hands in 30 BC. With Octavian (Augustus) being the sole remaining triumvir, the senate crowned him as Caesar Augustus Princeps, and emperor of Rome in 27 BC.

One of the first things that Augustus (Octavian) had to deal with was the stability of his eastern boarders. With Mark Antony having been a common enemy of both Augustus and Phraates IV, the two new leaders – in both Rome and Parthia – shared some common ground, around which a deal could be negotiated. Augustus decided that diplomacy was the order of the day, and so a deputation set out from Rome on the long journey to Parthia, bearing some precious tributes and tasked with seeking an alliance with King Phraates. One of the presents given to Phraates IV was a mysterious but very special lady, and she is central to this story.

II

Thea Muse Ourania

The year is 30 BC. Following the great naval battle of Actium, Antony and Cleopatra were dead and Octavian Augustus now presided over a unified Roman Empire that stretched from northern France to Upper Egypt, and from western Spain to the borders of Parthia (Persia). He was sole master of all he surveyed, with only one possible rival to his throne – the young son born of Julius Caesar and Cleopatra, Caesarion, who was already being hailed as the rightful pharaoh of Egypt. As a matter of political expediency, Augustus had him murdered. In the autumn of 30 BC Augustus left Egypt for Syria, to 'settle the affairs of the east'. En route he bestowed Cleopatra's personal bodyguard of Galatians upon a grateful King Herod the Great, who had skilfully (or luckily) dodged the shifting political allegiances in the region and remained in power as a client king of Rome.

The reason for Augustus' prolonged stay in Syria was most probably due to this being his most troublesome border. King Artaxes of Armenia had attacked King Artavasdes of Media. Phraates IV of Parthia had been deposed by an upstart prince called Tiridates. But Phraates IV was restored to the throne with the aid of the Scythians, and Tiridates fled to the Romans. Tiridates was most probably a Parthian prince, as the name Tiridates means 'Great Archer' in Persian, and the reverse of most Parthian coins portray an archer.

In short, there was a general sense of turmoil in the region, and all the parties in these diverse disputes looked towards Rome for military assistance. In fact, it is not difficult to see Augustus' hand behind the uprising in Parthia by Tiridates. It suited Augustus to have Parthia under his control, but Parthia had already proven itself an intractable nation to take by sheer military force, since it had already inflicted two great defeats upon the supposedly invincible Roman army. What better method than to take control of Parthia through a puppet prince, who would thereafter always be grateful to Rome for their assistance and support. However, whatever the cause of the insurrection, Phraates was only exiled from Parthia until 26 BC, when he made a successful return to power with the assistance of his Scythian allies.

Following this protracted stay in Syria, Augustus may then have briefly visited Greece before finally returning to Rome in August 29 BC to celebrate his various triumphs. There he had Cleopatra's other children by Mark Antony – twins Alexander Helios and Cleopatra Selene, and Ptolemy Philadelphus – paraded through the streets of Rome. The children were just ten and four years old respectively, and it is said that the golden chains they had to wear were so heavy they could hardly lift them. But, following this ritual humiliation, Augustus was magnanimous to the young children and they were all raised with Livia and Octavia, Augustus' wife and his sister respectively, in a household full of various imperial orphans.

Jubba II

Although we know that Cleopatra's children were looked after by Augustus and Octavia, we don't know what happened to them all, as nothing more is heard of the male children. It is unlikely that they were murdered, like Caesarion was, as Augustus had already spared their lives and raised them in his household. However, it is also unlikely that they survived into adulthood, as they would surely have been mentioned in one historical account or another. The only child of Cleopatra we do know about is Cleopatra Selene, who was given as a diplomatic bride to King Jubba II of Mauretania.

In fact, King Jubba (Iuba) had a lot in common with Selene, as he was also lucky to have survived the turmoil of the previous decades. His father had backed the wrong horse during the Roman civil war between Julius Caesar and Pompey, and so the captured king and his son were paraded through Rome as captives of Julius Caesar. King Jubba I had to endure five years of a Roman jail before being publicly beheaded; but his son was spared and became a friend of the young Octavian-Augustus. When Octavian became emperor, he reinstated his old playmate as King Jubba II of Mauretania (Numidia) in 25 BC, and to complete this royal appointment he gave Jubba the young princess Cleopatra Selene of Egypt as his bride.

Now this bridal match was quite a coup for the 25-year-old Jubba. Cleopatra Selene was an attractive teenager, she was the daughter of one of the most famous monarchs in that era, and she was also regarded as a manifestation of the goddess Isis. Selene must have brought great prestige to his small North African nation, and she certainly seems to have remained independent of her husband in many respects. Coins of Selene are always

Fig 4. Cleopatra Selene.

inscribed in her native Greek, as opposed to Jubba's coins which are marked in his adopted Latin. Their son was called Ptolemy, which demonstrates that Selene regarded her bloodline as being the superior. It is also suspected that their daughter was called Cleopatra.

Whatever the domestic politics of the Mauretanian royalty, the small nation seemed to remain stable and prosperous until Jubba's death in AD 23. After a long and successful reign, the couple were buried in a magnificent circular mausoleum known as the Kubr-er-Rumia (the Grave of the Roman Lady) by the Muslims and as the Tombeau de la Chrétienne (the Tomb of the Christian) by the French. [1] Note here that the tomb of Cleopatra Selene is being linked with Christianity, as this may be important in later chapters. The tomb is situated in modern Kolea, Algeria and unfortunately, due to the recent rise in Islamic fundamentalism, it is not possible to visit the area. However, the French did a number of surveys of the tomb back in the nineteenth century and these provide us with some interesting results.

Firstly, there is the overall design of the tomb. The tomb has a square base which supports a large, squat cylinder surrounded by sixty Ionic columns. Perched on the top of this is a conic pyramid, which has not been smoothed out but rather forms a series of small steps to the very top of the cone. This arrangement may look unusual and even unique, but this is not so. Further eastwards in Algeria at Batna, there is the Medracen Mausoleum, a monument whose history is unknown but whose design is strikingly familiar.

Likewise, if one travels eastwards across to the original hub of the Parthian empire, which is located to the east of the Caspian Sea in modern Turkmenistan, we find the Sultan Tekesh Mausoleum in Kunya Urgench. The history of this tomb is highly uncertain, as it predates the Mongolian invasions of this region in the thirteenth and fourteenth centuries, which destroyed the records and history of the kingdom. The tomb is thought to date from the eighth century Muslim period, but that is only a guestimation as the true ownership of this tomb is unknown and so an earlier date is entirely possible. Though smaller than the tomb of Cleopatra Selene, this mausoleum exhibits all of its attributes, including the square base, the cylindrical drum surrounded by columns and the conic roof structure. See the colour section for a comparison.

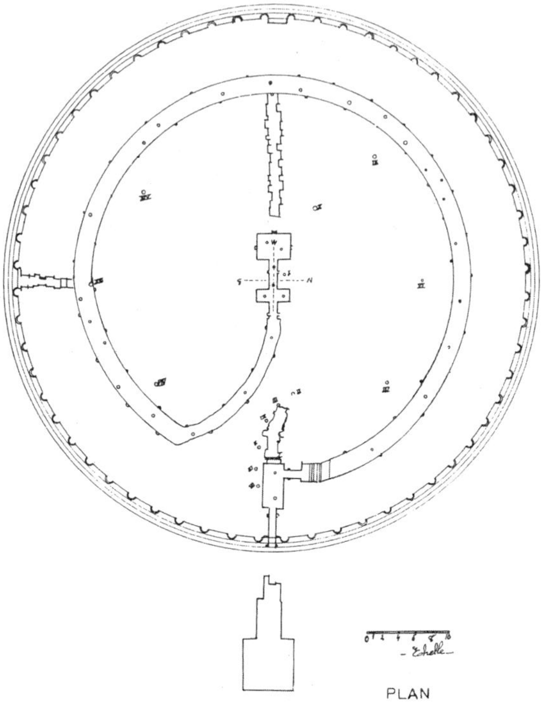

Fig 5. Plan view of the tomb of Jubba II and Cleopatra Selene.

While we might speculate that this similarity was a coincidence, based upon the desire to create a monument out of three mathematical structures in order to honour the Great Geometrician of the Universe, it is also possible that there were cultural links between Selene's North African Kingdom and Parthia, through which the mathematical understanding and technology for this type of design flowed. As we shall see shortly, those links may well have included a lost sister of Cleopatra Selene, who became queen of Parthia.

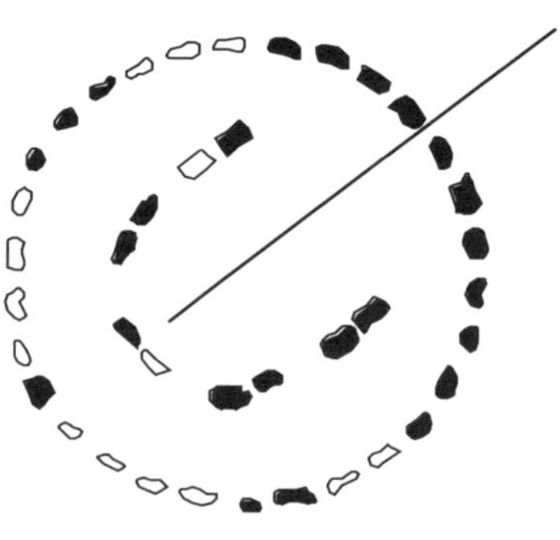

Fig 6. Outline of Stonehenge.

Whatever the method of transmission was for this design, its roots lie back in the very ancient past, in an era during which the properties of mathematics and astronomy were considered to be sacred in themselves. Indeed, if one would like to speculate freely, it is entirely possible that the design for Jubba and Selene's tomb was originally based upon the overall design of the Minorcan *talayots* and the geometry of Stonehenge.*

While this suggestion may sound a little bizarre, the form and design of these two monuments are somewhat similar. Selene's mausoleum exhibits sixty columns around its cylindrical base, instead of Stonehenge's thirty, but the general outline and the alignment to astronomical features is strikingly similar. It has already been proposed, by the puzzle designer and historical researcher Bruce Bedlam, that Stonehenge also once sported a conical roof structure; but since this would have been made of wood it has long since disappeared.

In addition, both of these monuments were purposely designed to include mathematical functions within their structure. The Stonehenge monument contains two prominent Pythagorean triangles within its layout, as I have explained in a previous work. Jubba and Selene's mausoleum is similar, in that the diameter of the lower cylinder is 60.85 m. This may not mean much, as we are using the wrong units, but since the drums of the columns that surround the tomb's lower cylinder each measure about 52 cm in height, I think we can safely say that this mausoleum was laid out in units of the Egyptian Thoth cubit (tc). (This is the Royal or Sacred cubit of Egypt, measuring 52.35 cm.) Bearing this in mind, the diameter of the lower cylinder of the mausoleum becomes 116.22 tc. While this length may not seem very illuminating either, if we multiply it by Pi (22 : 7) to get the circumference of the lower cylinder, the result is 365.25 tc – or the number of days in a year.

Fig 7. Stonehenge with conical roof structure (with thanks to Bruce Bedlam).

* See the colour section in the accompanying book *Scota* for a picture of the Minorcan *talayots*.

The reason for placing 60 columns around the lower cylinder of Jubba and Selene's tomb now becomes apparent. If we divide the circumference of the monument by 12, the result is 30.44 tc, or the number of days in a Solar month. Thus every five columns around the circumference of the tomb represents one month of the year. This identification with the Solar year means that Jubba II may have triumphed over his wife in the design of their last resting place. For Cleopatra Selene, whose name clearly identifies her with the Moon goddess, would no doubt have preferred 52 columns around the perimeter of her tomb – to represent the number of Lunar weeks in the year. (Four Lunar weeks equal a Lunar month, and so there are 13 Lunar months in the year.) Jubba II would have been represented by the male aspect of Helios, the Sun, as indeed was Selene's brother, Alexander Helios; while Selene herself would have been represented by the changeable female aspect of the Moon. Thus it would initially appear that the mausoleum was built to honour the Sun-god (Helios, Mithras, Ra, Aton, Amen), whom Jubba II no doubt revered.

However, this fine mausoleum is a deliberate blend of geometrical forms, and we have not yet looked at the cone-shaped pyramid upon its summit. Unfortunately, as with the Giza pyramids, this aspect of the monument was the first to be pillaged for its stones during the Islamic era, and most of the references to the height of the cone are taken from its present height. Since I have not yet found an accurate inclination for the cone, its original height is difficult to ascertain. However, from an analysis of pictures, and from estimating the number of missing layers to the cone, my best guess is that the inclination was originally 41 degrees and the original number of steps was originally 47. The height of each step is said to be 0.58 m, or 1.1 tc, and this would make the original cone 52 tc high, a number representing the Lunar weeks in the year.

It would be interesting to see if this is correct; for if it is, then it would seem that the female Lunar aspect of Selene was also honoured within the same monument. Within the design of the mausoleum, the two geometric figures of cylinder and cone honour the Great Geometrician of the Universe (god), while their measurements honour the Sun and Moon. Thus the diktats of traditional Egyptian dualism are preserved and honoured, and the royal couple of Mauretania become conjoined in death as Sun and Moon together.

Phraates

The marriage of Cleopatra Selene and Jubba II was celebrated in about 25 BC, and it was at about this time that Phraates IV unexpectedly regained the throne of Parthia, with the assistance of the Scythians; while the upstart Prince (King) Tiridates fled to Rome. Augustus, who had probably backed Tiridates in the first place, was not in a position to do much about this and must have decided to offer a hand of friendship to the Parthians instead of meddling further in their politics. However, this olive branch was hampered by Augustus' refusal to return the rebel prince / king (Tiridates) to Parthia, so that he could be dealt with by King Phraates. This Roman loyalty to the rebel prince (and king) again suggests that Augustus had backed his bid for the Parthian throne.

Faced with possible Parthian anger over his harbouring a renegade prince, Augustus had to do something to placate Phraates IV. There was also the small matter of the captured Roman standards to deal with. In the battles with Parthia that preceded his reign, Rome had lost two of its military standards, one by Crassus in 53 BC and the other by Mark Antony in 36 BC. These standards were powerful totems to the people of Rome in general and to the military establishment in particular, and Augustus knew that he would achieve a small symbolic victory just for having these all-important standards returned.

Augustus therefore had two problems to deal with in regard to Parthia and, with a military campaign out of the question, the only other option was diplomacy. It was for these reasons that Augustus sent various gifts to Phraates IV, to ease the tensions between the two great powers. Strangely enough, these gifts included the presentation of an 'Italian concubine' by the name of Thermusa, who was given as a personal chattel to Phraates IV. However, there is a great mystery here, for all of the contemporary historians, bar one, are totally silent on the subject of this mysterious lady. Yet, this lady was no common whore, who was being passed around the various rulers of the empire, for this lady rapidly became queen of Parthia and Phraates' chief wife.

The only historian who does venture to mention this lady is our old friend Josephus Flavius, the Jewish historian. But such was the deafening silence from all the other commentators and historians of this era, that Josephus' ribald tale about Thermusa and her son became another example of his 'unreliability' as a historian. That was, of course, until Parthian coins with Thermusa's image and name on them started turning up in the east; causing a minor flurry of historical embarrassment. It is my belief that many modern authorities like to champion Josephus Flavius' supposed 'unreliability' as a historian because his accounts clash strongly at times with the biblical narrative. However, more often than not it is Josephus' accounts that are correct, and it is the biblical accounts that are wrong. Josephus says of this mysterious and curiously unmentionable lady:

> Phraates ... had a love affair with an Italian concubine whose name was Thermusa, who had been formally sent to him amongst other presents by Julius Caesar. He first made her his concubine, but he being a great admirer of her beauty, and in the process having a son by her whose name was Phraataces, he made her his legitimate wife. [J2]

Thermusa did not simply become King Phraates' wife, she actually became his chief wife, and so her son became next in line for the throne. But how was this achieved? How did a common 'concubine' supersede the legitimate bloodline wives of Parthia? The answer is probably to be found in the example of King David, who similarly made a common soldier's wife, Bathsheba, his chief wife. In a similar fashion to Thermusa, it was through this 'commoner' that the great King Solomon was born. With the bloodline of the royals being of paramount importance, I did not believe this biblical tale at all, and thus I comprehensively demonstrated in the book *Solomon* that Bathsheba was no commoner at all. The lady was called Bath-Sheba בת-שבע, which means the Daughter of Sheba, and when she married the king (her father) she became the Queen of Sheba.

The tale is more complex than this, but it is as certain as anything can be in the Torah (or Tanakh) that Bathsheba was of royal blood, and the daughter of the king she married. Given her rapid rise to power and influence, it is likely that Thermusa was royal too, and in order to discover the necessary evidence we need to look more closely at her brief history.

Firstly, Josephus is wrong about the sender of this gift, for it was Augustus Caesar and not Julius Caesar who sent her. We know this because Julius was dead before Phraates IV came to the throne. It is often said that this mistake was due to Augustus being called Gaius Octavian Caesar before he became emperor, while Julius was called Gaius Julius Caesar. While this is possible, it is also possible that Julius Caesar did 'send' Thermusa in some fashion –□ because she may well have been his daughter

Secondly, this lady could not have been a simple 'Italian concubine'. This was a diplomatic gift from one of the most powerful leaders in the world at that time to another. Would Augustus Caesar have chosen a low-born concubine as a gift for King Phraates IV? Of course not. When Augustus sent a gift to Jubba II, the king of Mauretania, he gave him Cleopatra Selene, the daughter of Queen Cleopatra VII of Egypt (by Mark Antony). But Jubba II was another of the minnows of Roman geopolitics at that time, so why in this case did Jubba get an Egyptian princess while Phraates IV, king of all Parthia (Persia), was presented with an 'Italian concubine'?

If Thermusa was a concubine, then this was not a diplomatic gift and a token of respect by Augustus – but a bold diplomatic snub to the

Parthian king, and the result would have been a declaration of war on Rome. But no, Phraates was so impressed with his lowly 'concubine' that he made her his chief wife and later proceeded to make several risky political manoeuvres in order to make her son first in line for the Parthian throne.

So who was the mysterious Thermusa who so charmed Phraates IV? When looking at this situation from this new perspective, one reason for Thermusa being called a 'concubine' or 'slave' may be that the Parthians considered a hostage to be a 'slave'. This alternative view is apparent when Josephus narrates the return of a son of Phraates IV to Parthia, after being taken hostage by Rome for a number of years:

> Vonones was preferred above the rest and sent to them ... However, they soon changed their minds ... for they could not think of obeying the commands of one who had been a slave (for so they called those who had been hostages). [J3]

Thermusa had most definitely been a hostage of Rome, so perhaps this is one reason why she was called a 'concubine'. Nevertheless, considering Thermusa's meteoric rise to the position of chief wife of the king of Parthia (Persia), it is clear that she was a very important lady, but who exactly was she? And if she was indeed so prestigious, then why were all the Roman historians so quiet about her background and ancestry? What was there to hide? And why was it that the only historian to mention her at all was a Jewish historian from Judaea? Is this latter point in any way significant?

Ides of March

Having considered all the possibilities, the early twentieth century researcher A J Bethell deduced that Thermusa must have been Cleopatra VII, the queen of Egypt herself. While it is possible that Cleopatra did not die by the traditional asp bite in 30 BC, it is difficult to see how her presence in Rome was kept quiet for 15 years, or of what use she would be to Rome. Moreover, I do not think that Cleopatra would have been quite the perfect match that King Phraates of Parthia was expecting. Cleopatra was born in 69 BC, which would have made her 44 years old by the time Augustus sent his gifts to Parthia. While Cleopatra VII would still have been a prestigious wife to the king, she may also have been past childbearing age; and in royal dynastic terms, there is little point in having a sacred royal bloodline that cannot reproduce itself. No, there are too many problems involved with this scenario, and so we must look elsewhere for an alternative genealogy for the mysterious Thermusa.

Another possibility for her ancestry is contained in the reports that were given after the death of Julius Caesar. After Julius and Cleopatra's cruise down the Nile, Julius had some urgent campaigning to do in Bithynia, where he defeated Pharnaces II with ease in 47 BC. It wasn't until the summer of 46 BC that Julius and Cleopatra were able to meet up in Rome and for Cleopatra to make her grand entry into the city, as depicted in Joseph Mankiewicz's epic film, starring Elizabeth Taylor. Many historians doubt this extravagant portrayal, but considering the ostentatious and lavish royal court in which Cleopatra lived, I have no doubt that Cleopatra would have enjoyed making as much of a spectacle as was humanly possible.

Cleopatra and the infant Caesarion were then installed in the Trastevere, Julius Caesar's villa on the trans-Tiber. This caused an amount of scandal, because Calpurnia, Julius' wife, was being forced to house her husband's foreign mistress and their child. In fact, so bold was Julius that rumours circulated that he was going to marry Cleopatra, which would have entailed a change in the law because polygamy was not allowed in ancient Rome. Nevertheless, Julius and Cleopatra did live together in Rome as a pseudo 'king and queen' of the Roman Empire. But just as the rumours started to escalate, Julius was off to quell an uprising in Spain and did not return until the autumn of 45 BC, while Cleopatra made herself at home in Julius' Trastevere villa.

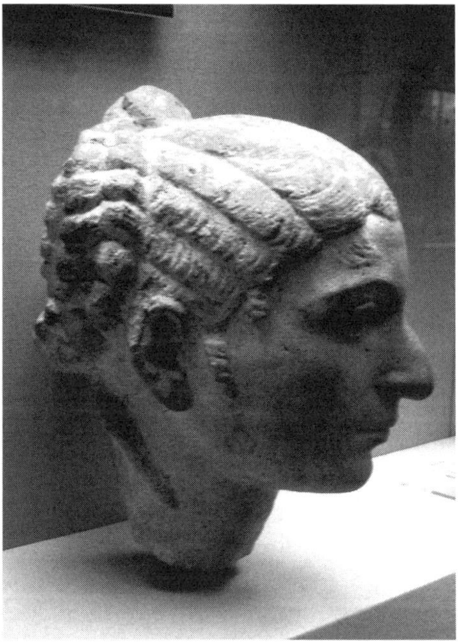

Fig 10. Bust of Cleopatra VII.

The historian Prof Erich Gruen doubts that Cleopatra could have stayed so long in Rome, as Egypt could not have remained stable without her presence. But I think that this view ignores Cleopatra's strategy and the balance of military power in the region. Egypt was rich in resources, especially gold and food, but she was militarily weak. Rome was desperate for resources but conversely had produced the most formidable army ever seen on the European continent. Cleopatra's position as queen of Egypt was safe as long as she was the mistress (or 'queen') of Julius Caesar – for if she were to be deposed, the new pretender to the throne of Egypt would have to answer to Caesar and to Rome. This was a formidable deterrent to any potential uprising in Egypt; as Professor Macurdy says:

> With Arsinoe (Cleopatra's sister) in Rome (as a captive) and Ptolemy XIII (her brother) drowned in the Nile, the young queen (Cleopatra VII) had little to fear so long as she had at her side the greatest Roman of the moment. [4]

Prof Gruen also doubts the story by the historian Appian that Julius Caesar placed a statue of Cleopatra in the Temple of Venus Genetrix, next to the Roman goddess, and that it survived into the reign of Augustus. Why, he asks, should a statue of a deposed foreign queen still receive veneration in a Roman temple dedicated to Venus? Actually, Appian may have been correct in his assertion, because Venus was the Greek Aphrodite, who was Phoenician Astarte, who was in turn the Egyptian Ast or Isis. Similarly, Cleopatra was also considered to be an incarnation of Isis, as were all of the Ptolemaic queens of Egypt, and so this statue in the Temple of Venus may have been a generic statue dedicated to Isis. Thus the two statues in the Temple may well have been different manifestations of the same goddess, and perhaps in this we see a reason why the people of Rome accepted Cleopatra so easily.

Fig 11. Isis and Horus, Madonna and Child.

The common people may have wanted to keep the statue because, as I have shown in my previous works, Isis – the archetypal mother goddess – was a very influential deity in the ancient world. So influential was she that she became the template for the Christian Madonna and Child. The Christian feast of Easter was also taken directly from the feast of Isis; indeed the name Easter was taken directly from the Egyptian name for Isis, which was Ast or Est . Cleopatra was considered by many to be an incarnation of Isis, and so the people may well have seen Cleopatra as Venus in earthly form. Who better to lead the Roman Empire than an exceptional army commander and a goddess.

Cleopatra was not only safe in Rome, she was also quietly plotting an Egyptian takeover of the Roman empire. To

Rome, which was a patrilineal society, Caesarion, Caesar's child by Cleopatra, was no particular national threat for the child was obviously Roman. But to Egypt, which was a matrilineal society, Caesarion was quite obviously an Egyptian prince, not a Roman successor. Had Cleopatra been able to manoeuvre Caesarion into being Julius Caesar's legal successor, her Egyptian takeover of Rome from within would have been complete. But, strange as it may seem, Julius never publicly acknowledged Caesarion as his son, and neither did he acknowledge him as his successor in his will. [5]

This omission is rather strange, and has provoked much speculation as to whether the child was actually his. But since Julius and Cleopatra were on their Nile cruise together at the critical time, it would seem difficult for the child to be anyone's but Caesar's, and so it has been speculated that Julius did not want to create a civil war by providing Rome with a highly contentious half-Egyptian successor. The recent epic BBC television series, 'Rome', dealt with this very topic, and the view of the historical producers of this series was that a lowly foot-soldier was responsible for Caesarion – although, in being a popularist series, this may well represent another element of added spice to the story-line. However, this scenario would indeed explain Julius' strange failure to acknowledge Caesarion as his heir.

In the autumn of 45 BC Julius returned from Spain to take up residence once more with Cleopatra, but the politics of the era were conspiring against him. A faction was conspiring to proclaim Julius as king of the Roman Empire, and it is difficult not to see Julius' hand acting quietly behind the scenes to promote this conspiracy. Julius Caesar, as king of the Roman Empire, would have needed a queen of royal blood to consummate the royal union, and who else but Cleopatra would have been his first choice? Accordingly, at the festival of Lupercalia, Mark Antony stepped up onto the rostrum to place a royal diadem (or crown) upon Julius Caesar's head to proclaim him as king. But instead of adulation, the crowds remained silent and, judging the mood of the populous in an instant, Julius pushed the diadem away from his head and proclaimed that only the god Jupiter could be king of Rome. The crowds roared their approval of this. Clearly, now was not the time to be assuming royal pretensions.

However, many in the Senate were now convinced that Julius did indeed want to be king, and that his choice of queen would be Cleopatra of Egypt and not his legal wife, Calpurnia. It was for this reason that, come the fateful day of 15th March 44 BC – the Ides of March – Julius Caesar was assassinated by a group of senators, including Marcus Junius Brutus. In an instant, all of Cleopatra's careful planning and intrigues had been dashed. Her protector had gone, and her child had not been named as Julius Caesar's heir. She was not only now in danger from the Roman squabbles over a new emperor, but the protection she had enjoyed from potential pretenders to the throne in Egypt had also evaporated. There was nothing else she could do but flee back to Egypt as fast as possible, to stabilise her position there. This she did, and that may well have been the end of the story, but as she left Rome a number of curious remarks were penned by Cicero:

> The rumour about the queen (Cleopatra) is losing strength.
>
> I would like to know the truth about the queen (Cleopatra) and about that Caesar too.
>
> I would like the story about the queen (Cleopatra) to be true. [6]

Clearly there was a great rumour circulating about Cleopatra before she left Rome for Egypt, but what exactly were these covert whisperings all about? Well, it would seem that there was a strong rumour about 'that Caesar', but the rumour then diminished for some reason. The Caesar in question is unlikely to have been Julius, as he was now dead. Instead, the rumour may have been related to Caesarion's disputed paternity; but since Caesarion was not mentioned in Julius' will, that particular rumour was now largely irrelevant – it was highly unlikely that Caesarion could now become the next emperor. Likewise, the rumour is again unlikely to have been about Caesarion, as Julius Caesar's son was clearly known by the diminutive form of Caesar, which is clearly a different title. So who was this new Caesar? Why the intrigue and why did the rumour diminish with time?

It is entirely possible that the answer to this is to be found in the later comments penned by Cicero. It is said that he opined:

> Writing to Atticus on 10 May 44. After expressing sorrow at hearing of a miscarriage, Cicero says that he hopes or wishes that 'it may be true' about the queen (Cleopatra) and 'that Caesar of hers'. [7]

A direct translation of Cicero's letter reads:

> I am grieved to hear of Tertia's loss of an expected child ... (but) I should be glad of such a loss in the case of the queen (Cleopatra) and that [expected] scion of the breed of Caesar. [8] (Author's brackets.)

It would seem that the persistent rumour floating around Rome when Julius Caesar was assassinated was that Cleopatra was pregnant. So the import of Cicero's letter is that he is secretly hoping that Cleopatra also has a miscarriage, just like Tertia had had recently. The unknown 'Caesar' who he was alluding to in his earlier letter may therefore have been Cleopatra's unborn second child – a child who would have been most certainly fathered by Julius Caesar. And since Cicero mentions a scion or heir, and Rome was a patrilineal society, Cleopatra must have been desperately hoping for a son.

This pregnancy may sound unlikely, bearing in mind the almost total lack of historical commentary on this matter, but actually it is not such a dubious suggestion. Julius had returned from Spain in the autumn of 45 BC, and he was not assassinated until the spring of 44. Meanwhile, Cleopatra was living openly in his trans-Tiber villa as the emperor's mistress. Even if Julius did have another mistress in Spain, it was always the soldier's solemn duty to re-consummate a relationship upon his return from an expedition, and it is therefore a certainty that Julius and Cleopatra slept together and had conjugal relations once more in the autumn of 45. Julius' seeming lack of virility aside, the possible pregnancy of Cleopatra that Cicero alludes to is therefore more likely than unlikely.

However, following Julius' death, Cleopatra and Caesarion (and the unborn child) were highly vulnerable. In the circumstances, Cleopatra's most potent form of defence against the senators who had murdered Julius Caesar (and against her other enemies in Rome) would be to go to a reputable seer and divine the sex of her unborn child – for if it was a boy it would have a strong claim to become the next emperor, much more so than the unfortunate Caesarion. Caesarion was of unknown parentage – he had arrived in Rome as an infant and Julius had pointedly failed to acknowledge him as his son, for whatever reason. What were the Romans to think? This new pregnancy was, however, conceived in the limited confines of the Trastevere villa, and everyone knew that the only possible father was Julius Caesar himself. Who would dare murder the Queen of Egypt and the unborn true heir to the Roman Empire?

Thus Cleopatra's first move was to go straight to the temple – most probably the Temple of Venus that contained her own statue. The nervous priestess and seer who Cleopatra consulted, being faced with a 50 - 50 chance and a tempting pot of gold, said that her unborn child was most definitely a boy. This was 'that Caesar' that Cicero was alluding to, and this was the reason for his wanting Cleopatra to have a miscarriage. A new contender to the throne of the Empire at this late stage would have upset the entire apple cart, and possibly led to civil unrest, as well as ensuring that an Egyptian prince became emperor.

But the crisis was soon over, and the rumour 'lost strength'. Why? Well, if Cleopatra had conceived this new child in the September or October of 45 BC, then the child would have been born in the May or June of 44. In other words, the baby could have been due very shortly after Cicero's second letter was written. Cleopatra was hoping for a boy, but if the seer guessed wrongly and the child was a girl, then Cicero would have been most happy. This was the story that he wanted to be true, and this is the reason for the rumour about Cleopatra's 'Caesar' losing its strength.

Despite this obviously being a worrying subject for the contemporary historians, which was clouded in much secrecy and intrigue, there is one other allusion to Cleopatra's second pregnancy by Julius Caesar. A coin was discovered with the image of Cleopatra suckling a child, which is usually interpreted as being the infant Caesarion. However, the coin also contains the legend 'Kupr', the name for the island of Cyprus, and so the coin is indicating that Cleopatra was ruling Cyprus at the time. [9]

P J Bicknell and others have argued that Cleopatra did not gain control over Cyprus until 44 or 43 BC. But Caesarion was born in 47 BC, which would have made him too old to be a suckling infant at this time. To explain this strange anomaly away, it has been argued that this image on the coin was therefore representative of Cleopatra's incarnation of the Egyptian goddess Isis, and thus the representation is therefore the standard icon of Isis and her son Horus. However, while that is possible, the image may also be that of Cleopatra and her new daughter by the late Julius Caesar.

So is this phantom child simply my own conjecture, or is there any substance to these rumours and speculations? Well, the translation of Cicero's letter by Prof Macurdy seems to be self-explanatory; Cleopatra was pregnant shortly before the death of Julius Caesar, and I am certainly not alone in this speculation. The following are comments by historians who have been working closely in this field:

> However, it is quite likely, from Cicero, that Cleopatra was pregnant in late 45 or early 44. If this pregnancy was not Caesarion, then it presumably miscarried or resulted in a child who did not long survive birth. [12]

> Moreover, another child was the natural result of the continued union of Caesar and such a fecund woman as Cleopatra, who desired to have heirs for Caesar and the Roman-Egyptian empire. [13]

> Since the question of the paternity of (Cleopatra's) son Caesarion was to be hotly discussed in Rome, it seems not unlikely that Cleopatra would wish to have another child by Caesar at the time when she was living in his house, when there would be no doubt that Caesar was the father. [14]

But there was no further mention of this 'phantom' pregnancy. Was Cleopatra bluffing? Did she miscarry, as Cicero desired? While either of these suggestions are plausible, the most likely reason why the contemporary historians fell silent, on the topic of Cleopatra's second pregnancy through Julius Caesar, is that the pregnancy resulted in an unexpected and unwanted daughter. No accounts were written about this child because she was of no benefit to anyone, and a great disappointment to Queen Cleopatra herself. Cleopatra already had an heir to Egypt – her son Caesarion – what she did not have was an indisputable male heir to Rome, born of Julius Caesar. The new daughter could not be this heir because Rome was a patrilineal society with a patrilineal ruling class. In short, Cleopatra's unwanted and rejected daughter probably became one of many royal children in this era who slipped into obscurity, as did her later sons by Mark Antony. However, that obscurity was not to last forever.

New generation

We now move on a decade or so. After Julius' murder, Cleopatra had allied herself with one of his successors, Marcus Antonius or Mark Antony. Together, the couple controlled the south and east of the Roman Empire, and together they had three children; a twin daughter and son who were named Cleopatra Selene and Alexander Helios, and another son called Ptolemy. But Cleopatra's dreams of taking over the whole of the Roman Empire were again to be shattered, and following the defeat of Mark Antony at the great sea-battle of Actium, Augustus (Octavian) pursued Antony and Cleopatra back to Egypt in late 31 BC.

Egypt effectively capitulated to the Romans at this point in time and lost its independence completely. After it was explained to Cleopatra that she would be a central part of the victory parade in Rome, to be dragged through the streets shackled in golden chains, she chose to kill herself instead. With the Roman empire now controlling all of Egypt, Augustus took all of Cleopatra's children to Rome to celebrate his triumph, in which they were indeed paraded in golden chains. These included Selene, Helios and Ptolemy, but was there an older fourth child too?

Back in Rome, Augustus took his time sorting out the loose ends of his empire. As was mentioned previously, to strengthen his position in North Africa, Augustus decided to give his old friend Jubba II the teenage daughter of Cleopatra VII, Cleopatra Selene, as wife and queen. With his southern border secure in the hands of a loyal client-king, Augustus now looked towards the east, where Phraates IV has just retaken his throne from the upstart Parthian prince, Tiridates. In order to placate King Phraates and cement a lasting alliance with the powerful Parthian empire, he needed to give Phraates something special, something that would demonstrate Rome's respect for Parthia and Augustus' desire for a lasting peace and friendship between these two great empires. Jubba II had already been given the hand of Cleopatra VII's daughter in marriage, and so the mighty King Phraates IV would need something much more prestigious than this. What Augustus does, is to give King Phraates an Italian concubine called Thermusa. Jubba II, the minnow of Mauretania, gets a princess and goddess of Egypt, while King Phraates IV of all Parthia gets a whore!

Thea Muse

As has already been laboured at some length, for this diplomatic offering to make any sense, quite plainly Thermusa could not have been a common concubine and must have been a royal princess of some stature and breeding. In the circumstances, she can only have been the long-forgotten 19-year-old daughter of Cleopatra VII and Julius Caesar, who would have been in her prime for bearing Phraates sons and daughters of royal and sacred Egyptian blood. While this deduction may seem like a leap of faith at this stage, there are many reasons for thinking that this is true.

Firstly, it is an established fact that Egyptian princesses had already been given to the kings of Parthia. During the New Kingdom era such diplomatic marriages were forbidden, as Egyptian princesses were never given to foreign kings. However, the Egyptian Ptolemaic dynasty sent many a princess to Persia, as the two royal families shared a common Greek heritage during this era. It was in this manner that in 150 BC a certain princess called Cleopatra Thea became the wife of three Seleucid kings: Alexander Balas, Demetrius II and Antiochus VII. The Seleucid empire was founded by one of Alexander the Great's generals, Seleucus, and at its height it controlled all of the Persian lands. However, by the reign of Alexander Balas the ruling Seleucid dynasty had become unstable and it was soon to be eclipsed by the growing might of the Parthian Arsacid dynasty. But if the Seleucid dynasty could be blessed with a dynastic alliance with the royal line of Egypt, then why not the Parthian Arsacid dynasty too?

Secondly, there is the interesting matter of the names of Phraates' wives. A document known as the Second Avroman Parchment records the wives of Phraates IV in 20 BC, just five years after the gift of Thermusa to King Phraates IV. It gives their names as being Olenieire, Baseirta, Bistheibanaps and Cleopatra. [15] This last name is odd, because while an Egyptian princess called Cleopatra Thea had married into the Seleucid dynasty, there is no trace of a dynastic alliance between Egypt and the Parthian Arsacid dynasty. So where did this wife called Cleopatra come from? I think the obvious answer is that Thermusa was only a nickname for this princess, and her real name would have been Cleopatra, because in reality she was Cleopatra's daughter. Cleopatra VII's second daughter was called Cleopatra Selene, and so it is likely that any daughter by Julius Caesar would have been named likewise.

Thirdly, even the name Thermusa contains echoes of the Egyptian queen, Cleopatra. The full title of this 'Italian concubine' was Thea Muse Ourania, meaning 'Goddess Muse Ourania' (more accurately pronounced as Thea Musa Ourania in the Greek). In Greek mythology Ourania was actually the Greek *muse*, or inspirational goddess, of astronomy and since Ourania was in charge of the heavens she was often considered to be the Muse of Heaven, or the Muse of the Stars. In fact, the name Ourania was derived from ouranos ουρανος meaning 'heaven', and so a literal translation of Thea Muse Ourania would be 'Goddess of Heaven' or, by implication, the 'Queen of Heaven'.

But Ourania was not the original Queen of Heaven, for that title must surely go to the Egyptian Isis. In the second century AD, Lucius Apuleius had a vision of Isis, who described herself as:

> I am she that is the natural mother of all things, mistress and governess of all the elements, the initial progeny of worlds, chief of powers divine, Queen of Heaven, the principal of the Gods celestial, the light of the goddesses: at my will the planets of the air, the wholesome winds of the Seas, and the silences of hell be disposed; my name, my divinity is adored throughout all the world in divers manners, in variable customs and in many names ... the Egyptians ... do call me Queen Isis. [16]

Isis was not, of course, the only Queen of Heaven, and so we find that there were a succession of goddesses who were manifestations of Isis. The name of the Phoenician goddess Astarte, for instance, has been taken directly from the Egyptian Ast or Est , which was the original Egyptian name for Isis. So it should not be a surprise that Astarte is then described in the *Encyclopaedia Britannica* as being the Queen of Heaven, for she was indeed the Phoenician Isis. In her turn, the Phoenician Astarte can be seen as an ancestor of the Greek Aphrodite, the goddess of love, and Selene, the goddess of the Moon. This is why Muse Ourania was also sometimes called Venus Ourania, because she was so closely associated with Venus-Aphrodite.

Since all of the Ptolemaic queens of Egypt modelled themselves upon the goddess Isis, many of these names and titles display a great deal of synergy with Queen Cleopatra VII. Likewise, since Isis was known as the Queen of Heaven, Cleopatra VII named her twins (by Mark Antony) Alexander Helios and Cleopatra Selene, or Alexander Sun and Cleopatra Moon. As she was now the mother of the Sun and the Moon, Thea Muse Cleo-Patra (Cleopatra VII) could just as easily have been recognised as being Thea Muse Ourania, the Goddess of the Heavens.

We have no idea what Cleopatra VII's second child (by Julius Caesar) may have been called, but Thea Muse Ourania (Josephus' Thermusa) would have been a distinctly appropriate title, if only as a hypocorism or nickname.

Fourthly, the name of the pharaoh's daughter, who supposedly found the infant biblical Moses and brought up this child in the royal court of Egypt, was called Thermuthis. [J17] Several theologians have seen in this name a hint of the pharaonic name Tuthmoses, and have tried to make links accordingly. However, the Egyptian version of this same name was actually known as Renenutet  , and the link to Josephus' princess called Thermuthis lies in the fact that the Greek name for Renenutet was Thermuthis. Now Renenutet was a fertility goddess in the guise of a serpent, and she was strongly linked to the goddess Isis. In other words, the Egyptian princess who reared Moses in the royal court was either called Renenutet-Isis, or she was being regarded as a personification of Renenutet-Isis. [18]

There is also a desperately awful pun being made here by Josephus' scribes, which certainly works in the English, and since the visual imagery would have been the same in all languages it should also work in the Greek or Hebrew. * The goddess Renenutet  was known as 'She who Rears Up', with the visual imagery here being the cobra rearing up ready to strike. But of course Josephus' *Antiquities* says that is was Princess Thermuthis who 'reared' the infant Moses, and so it could be said that she 'reared up' the child. A poor form of wit, I know, but the Egyptian texts are full of this predictable and not always witty repartee.

So what does the biblical Egyptian princess called Thermuthis have to do with Cleopatra and Thea Muse? Well, Cleopatra was also deemed to be a personification of the goddess Isis, as were all the Ptolemaic queens, as we have seen. Isis was known as the Queen of Heaven, or perhaps the

* In the Hebrew the terms are *omnah* אמנה meaning 'raise' and *quwm* קום meaning 'rise'. Since both terms refer to something standing upright, the pun should also work in the Hebrew.

Queen of the Stars. This was a title held by many of the Egyptian and biblical royalty, including the Queen of Sheba, whose name can be literally translated in the Egyptian as being the 'Queen of the Stars'. In addition, the goddess Renenutet, or Thermuthis, was said to be the image of Isis in the guise of a cobra; while in a similar fashion it was said that Cleopatra was bitten by an asp (although most modern biologists indicate that the Egyptian cobra would have been the preferred reptile). So Princess Thermuthis and Queen Cleopatra were both closely associated with Isis and also with a snake.

It was most probably for this reason that Josephus Flavius managed to turn the name Thea Muse into Thermusa, because the latter name is very similar indeed to the name of Thermuthis, the princess who found and reared Moses. His alteration seems to indicate that the 'Italian concubine' called Thea Muse can be equated both with an Egyptian princess and also with the goddess Isis, and if she were a daughter of Cleopatra VII then we can do just that.

Fifthly, Thea Muse Ourania can also be strongly linked with the Greek Aphrodite, the goddess of love, who was simply a much later incarnation of the Egyptian Isis (Ast or Est ). In a similar fashion, Cleopatra VII's title was derived from the Greek terms *clio* and *patra.*

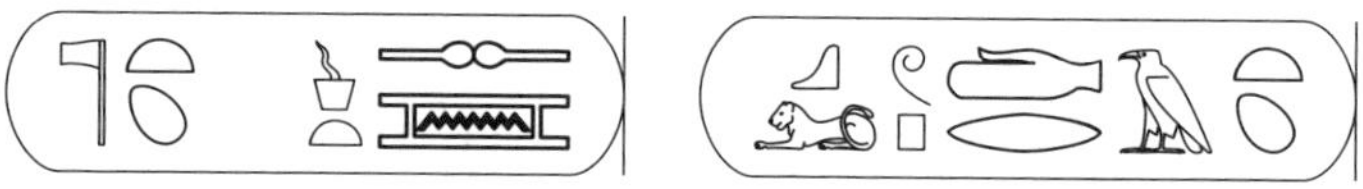

Neter-t Merites Cleopatra-t

Fig 12. Cartouches of Cleopatra VII.

The term *'clio'* is said to have been derived from the Greek *muse* Clio, the *muse* of poetry and history, which would result in a name meaning 'Poetical Muse of my Father'. However, the general opinion is that Cleo-Patra's title means 'Glory of my Father'. It is likely that this translation is mirrored in Cleopatra's Egyptian royal title, which was Neter-t Merites  which means 'Goddess Love of Father' or perhaps even 'She, the Goddess of Love'. By using the Greek term for 'goddess', Cleopatra's Egyptian name might then become 'Thea Aphrodite' or 'Goddess of Love', a fitting title for an incarnation of Isis.

Thus Thea Muse Cleo-Patra (Cleopatra VII) and Thea Muse Ourania seem to have had very similar titles in many respects. Both were named after the Greek muses, and both were named after the goddess Isis; so Thea Muse Ourania would have been a fitting hypocorism for the daughter of the great Egyptian queen.

Sixthly, Phraates IV and Thea Muse Ourania had at least two children that we know of. There was Phraates V, a son who was known as Phraataces (which is a diminutive of the name Phraates) and Julia Ourania. The reason why the latter is significant is to be found in the clan names of Rome. Julius' full name was Gaius Julius Caesar (or Caius Yulius Caesar). The term Julius showed that he was from the Julius family, or clan, and the name Caesar demonstrated that he was of the Caesar branch of that larger family. The term 'Caesar' meaning 'emperor' only came into vogue after Julius' reign.

Clan or family names were rigidly adhered to, much as the clan names in Scotland are, although it has to be said that slaves sometimes took the clanname of their master. However, here we have a princess of Parthia who has been given the name of the Julian family in Rome. So why was this done? If Thea Muse was simply giving her daughter the name of her Roman patron, then she should have been called Octavian (Augustus). The choice of the family name of Julius demonstrates once again that Thea Muse was related to Julius Caesar, as Josephus Flavius suspected – and indeed she *was* related to Julius because she was his daughter by Cleopatra VII.

Finally, there is the suggestion by the French historian, Settipani, that Julia Ourania married Ptolemy of Mauretania. Now if Thea Muse (Thermusa) was indeed a daughter of Cleopatra VII, then this would have been a strategic alliance between North Africa (Mauretania) and Persia (Parthia) that made every sense. The mother of Ptolemy of Mauretania was Cleopatra Selene, the daughter of Cleopatra VII, and so this possible marriage alliance between Ptolemy of Mauretania and Julia Ourania would have been a marriage of royal Egyptian cousins, both of whom were directly descended from Cleopatra VII. [19] It would seem unlikely that this alliance would have been arranged if Thea Muse were not a daughter of Cleopatra VII. (See the family tree in the appendix.)

The evidence suggests that a branch of the Ptolemaic royal line had been forcibly uprooted from Egypt, by Rome, and deposited in Parthia; where it appears to have taken root and prospered. But this story is not about Parthia, it is supposed to be about Judaea and the biblical accounts of the New

Testament. So how, in this case, does the mighty royal family of Parthia become involved in the events in Judaea that shaped modern Christianity? Well, the New Testament recounts a tale of turbulent times and some of this turbulence was about to strike the Parthian royal family.

III

Ourania and Aurania

A few years after the gift of Thea Muse to Phraates IV, in about 20 BC, Augustus journeyed to the east once more and reopened his friendly diplomacy with the Parthian king. The subject on Augustus' mind was the ongoing dispute about the Roman military standards, which had been captured by the Parthians in 53 and 36 BC. While it may seem a little strange to organise a diplomatic mission to retrieve a lost standard, or regimental colour, these standards were actually highly important elements of the Roman fighting machine. Indeed, an entire military campaign was organised in order to retrieve the standards lost by Varus in the Teutoburger Wald of Germany. Likewise, Mark Antony's 36 BC campaign into Parthia was spurred on by the prospect of retrieving a lost standard; but he only succeeded in losing yet another standard to the Parthians. Again, the BBC series 'Rome' dwelt on this very subject, and depicted Caesar's legions retrieving a lost standard in Gaul.

The standards themselves came in many guises, with early examples being an eagle, wolf, horse or boar. Only in later centuries was the design standardised around the *aquila* eagle design with the legend SPQR attached to it. These famous initials stand for *Senatus Populusque Romanus* or 'the Senate and the People of Rome', which was not exactly who the army were fighting for after Julius Caesar took the throne as emperor.

Having mentioned the military standards, it would be remiss not to look at the similar cult of the Roman *fasces*. One of the prime symbols of office for high dignitaries and for the emperor himself was the *fasces*, which comprised an axe secured within a bundle of rods and tied together with red tapes. Unfortunately, the origins and meaning of this design seem to have been completely lost to the Romans, let alone modern historians. However, if the reader will allow me the liberty of continuing my thesis that most of

Fig 16. A statue of Cincinnatus holding the Roman Fasces – from which we derive the word fascism.

Western civilisation seems to have sprung from Egypto-Judaic roots, the true meaning of the *fasces* can perhaps be divined. This is not simply a point of academic interest, as the *fasces* is still an important emblem today.

Since the *fasces* was carried by Roman court officials, the axe portion of the fasces is said to represent punishment – the ultimate judicial sanction of decapitation. However, it is much more likely that the axe was derived from the Egyptian god-axe , a symbol that was adopted by the influential Minoan empire, who no doubt transported it all over the Mediterranean during their extensive trading voyages. The Roman *fasces* is said to have originated with the Etruscans, and since the Etruscans were related to the Sea People alliance and to the later Phoenician empire, this would seem entirely reasonable. Instead of symbolising punishment, therefore, the axe would have represented divine power.

The bundle of rods that form the bulk of the *fasces* are again said to represent the sanction of punishment by the courts, with the criminal facing the possibility of being lashed. However, the true origin for the meaning of these rods can perhaps be glimpsed from the number of *fasces* that were carried before the various high officials, which were six, twelve or twenty-four, depending on their rank. This would suggest that the *fasces* pertained in some manner to the zodiac, or perhaps the twelve tribes of Israel. That the latter is the more likely can be clearly seen in a quote from Josephus:

> Moses only desired the heads of the tribes to bring their rods, with the names of their tribes inscribed upon them, and that he should receive the priesthood in whose rod god should give a sign. This was agreed to. So the rest brought their rods, as did Aaron also, who had written the tribe of Levi on his rod. These rods Moses laid up in the tabernacle of God. [J1]

Thus each of these rods symbolised, and was inscribed with, the name of a tribe of the Hyksos-Israelites. Thus it is likely that the twelve rods, had Moses tied them together in a *fasces,* would have been a symbol of unity between the often fractious Hyksos-Israelite tribes. Taken together, the axe and the rods would then represent the unity of the Hyksos-Israelite tribes and their being bound to the divine power of the one god, which was represented by the axe symbol. This argument would make sense of the available archaeological and epigraphic information about the *fasces,* but it would make the symbol's later usage rather incongruous.

The *fasces* was prominently used, for instance, by the German and Italian Fascists during the Second World War – indeed the term 'fascist' comes directly from the name of the *fasces* itself. However, it would now appear that the emblem of the Fascists was an Egypto-Judaic symbol – but only the most foolhardy of historians would have mentioned this to the Nazis.

Fig 17. The Lincoln Memorial in Washington. Lincoln's hands rest upon two fasces.

Notwithstanding the *fasces'* modern association with Fascism, it is still a widely used symbol of authority. It is used as an emblem by the Spanish police, for instance, and also for French passports; and it used to appear on the American dime coin. More interestingly, two prominent *fasces* form the armrests of the seat upon which Abraham Lincoln sits in the Lincoln Memorial. In other words, the authority of the American establishment is directly related to the authority of the Roman Senate, and perhaps before that to the authority of the Egyptian state. Finally, bearing in mind the Roman use of the *fasces* within their court system, the use of red tape for binding important court documents also, no doubt, stems from the design of the *fasces*.

Diplomacy

On this particular diplomatic mission to Parthia, Augustus was successful and the long-lost military standards were returned by the Parthians to Rome – on 12th May 20 BC to be precise, according to Gardthausen. [2] But what had caused this change of heart by the Parthians, after all this time? Augustus himself relates on the Ancyra Monument that:

> The Parthians I compelled to restore to me the spoils and standards of three Roman armies, and to seek as suppliants the friendship of the Roman people. These standards I deposited in the inner shrine which is in the Temple of Mars Ultor. [3]

Using a level of political spin worthy of Britain's current Labour Party, Augustus here infers that he forced the Parthians to return the standards by threats of force. However, Augustus was not in a position to threaten the Parthians, and so it is much more likely that this success was the result of Thea Muse's manipulation of her husband, the king. As Josephus says:

> Now (Thea Muse) was able to persuade (Phraates IV) to do anything that she said... [J4]

The reason for Thea Muse's assistance to Rome in this matter was that she was plotting a long-term strategy to ensure that her son became the next king of Parthia, and it was likely that she would need Roman assistance in this endeavour. She no doubt wrote to Augustus and promised the return of the standards, as he is highly unlikely to have made such a long journey to the east on the off-chance of a successful negotiation with Phraates IV. As far as Thea Muse was concerned, the *quid pro quo* was that Augustus would accept all of Phraates IV's other sons as hostages, leaving her son free to take the throne of Parthia when her husband died. Queen Thea Muse had been gifted to King Phraates in about 25 BC and so her son, Phraataces, may have been three or so years old by this time.

Whatever the case, Thea Muse's influence over the old king must have been complete, because he agreed to this bizarre proposition; and a few years after the return of the Roman standards, Phraates sent his four sons to Rome as hostages. It is often thought that Phraates may have been persuaded that his sons were plotting to depose him, and this is why he agreed to send them away to Rome. But to have not foreseen the devious designs of Thea Muse, in clearing the way for her son to be king, was a fatal mistake. Of course, Phraates may have wanted his youngest son, Phraataces, to take the throne, but not in the way that events transpired.

Augustus Caesar must have been delighted by this fortuitous outcome. He had not only recovered the lost military standards without firing so much as an arrow, but he could (and did) claim great political credit back in Rome for doing so. Florus and Strabo write of this eventuality:

> The Parthians, as if they repented of their victories, brought back of their own accord, the standards taken from Rome. [5]

> Phraates was so anxious to obtain the friendship of Augustus Caesar that he even sent the trophies. [S6]

Yes indeed. Phraates had been so anxious to placate Rome that he had held onto the military standards for 33 and 16 years respectively! Clearly, Phraates was in no hurry to placate Rome and so it is likely that the only friendship he wished to enhance was that of his domineering Romo-Egyptian wife, Thea Muse Ourania [Cleopatra II of Parthia].

In addition, Augustus must have been even more delighted that he now had the four princess of Parthia as hostages, which he could perhaps use as leverage at some point in the future. Augustus' current working relationship with Thea Muse was obviously cordial and mutually beneficial, but if things turned more sour he could always threaten to install one of his puppet princes on the throne of Parthia.

While the maverick (but reliable) historian Josephus Flavius pointedly states that the princes of Parthia were sent to Rome at the bidding of Thea Muse to allow her son to became king, the cautious Strabo takes the more orthodox line:

> (Phraates) was apprehensive of conspiracy and attempts on his life ... He therefore removed his sons out of the way with a view to annihilating the

> hopes of the disaffected ... The sons who live in Rome, are entertained as princes at the public expense. [S7]

It is true that the usurper from 29 BC, called Tiridates, had most probably been a Parthian prince; and it is true that many a king has been uncertain about his son's intentions; however, I still prefer Josephus' version of events. For one thing, the sending of these princes to Rome could only be seen as a sign of Parthian weakness, which would not look good on either the domestic or the international front. Conversely, it was also a propaganda coup for Augustus, who milked this 'victory' for all it was worth. Would Phraates really wanted to have an emboldened Rome on his doorstep, and possible rebellion at home, simply to remove a vague threat from his sons? Was there no other way of dealing with this situation?

On the Ancyra Monument Augustus Caesar writes:

> Phraates, son of Orodes, king of the Parthians, sent all his sons and grandsons to me in Italy, not because he had been conquered in war, but rather seeking our friendship by means of his own children as pledges. And a large number of other nations experienced the good faith of the Roman people during my principate who never before had had any interchange of embassies or of friendship with the Roman people. [8]

It is also a fact that King Phraates IV did not 'remove all his sons'. He removed all except Phraataces, the son of Thea Muse, and it was conveniently Phraataces who became the next king of Parthia. As Josephus said in a quote earlier in this chapter, Thea Muse was able to persuade Phraates to do anything. But this decision by King Phraates must once again call into question Thea Muse's supposed humble heritage. The sons who Phraates had sent to Rome were of the Arsacid dynasty, who had ruled Parthia since 250 BC. For Phraates to be sidelining this powerful and illustrious dynasty, in favour of a son through Thea Muse, indicates that her bloodline must have been even more famous and possibly sacred, and what other royal line than the Egyptian's could have achieved this?

King Phraates' bargain with Rome also implies that Rome was happy with Thea Muse's and Phraataces' royal credentials, and that Phraates IV himself trusted Rome not to interfere with Phraataces' succession. For Rome was now the baby-sitter to four of Parthia's most famous princes, and could have easily used these Arsacid princes to foment revolt and insurrection in Parthia. That Rome did not entertain this thought demonstrates a tacit acceptance of Phraataces' claim to the Parthian throne.

The presence of Phraates' four sons in Rome was also a veiled warning to the young Phraataces that he needed to be a wise and just ruler. For King Phraates had deliberately left his Arsacid sons in Rome, instead of ruthlessly disposing of them, so that Phraataces would always risk the introduction of pretenders to the throne, backed by the power of Rome. Thus the actions of King Phraates may not have been quite so bizarre after all, and he may instead have deliberately ensured that Parthia would remain at peace with Rome long after his own death.

Regicide

So, with the four sons of King Phraates IV safely out of the running for the Parthian throne, the only true winner in all respects was Thea Muse – who only had to wait for her husband to die for her and her offspring to inherit the entire Parthian empire. The only minor snag with this plan was that Phraates was proving to be a little uncooperative in this regard, and was intent on living a full and long life. The obvious answer to this problem was for Thea Muse to hasten her husband's departure from this world. Accordingly, it is thought that King Phraates was poisoned by Thea Muse in about AD 2. With her husband out of the way, Thea Muse proceeded to appoint herself as Queen of Parthia in a co-regency with her son. And in a bizarre twist to this plot, in order to seal this co-regency of Parthia, Thea Muse then married her son, Phraataces.

Josephus Flavius is the only historian to relate these facts to us and, as I said before, his lurid accounts of this court intrigue were dismissed out of hand – until coins bearing the name of Thea Muse Ourania started turning up in Iran. But these were not simply coins of Thea Muse; instead, they come complete with the image of her son, Phraataces, on the reverse – with their images being titled 'king' and 'queen'. The full account of this intrigue, as narrated by Josephus Flavius, is as follows:

> Phraates, king of the Parthians died at about this time as a result of a conspiracy led by his son Phraataces, which began for the following reason. Phraates, when he already had legitimate sons, fell in love with an Italian slave girl named Thermusa, who had been sent, along with other gifts, by Julius Caesar. At first he treated her as a concubine, but with the passing of time, he was so taken by her beauty, and after she had a son named Phraataces, he declared her his lawful wife and held her in honor. When she achieved such influence that the king would do whatever she said, she, eager to obtain the kingship of the Parthians for a son to whom she had given birth, realized that she could only obtain her desire by contriving the removal of the legitimate children of the Parthian king,

> convinced him to send the legitimate children to Rome as hostages. They were sent to Rome, because it was not easy for Phraates (IV) to refuse the commands of Thermusa.
>
> Phraataces, who was alone being prepared for the throne, considered it a dangerous and tedious thing to take power handed over by his father; so he plotted, with the assistance of his mother, to do away with his father. There is also a story that he had sexual relations with her. He was detested for both reasons, since his subjects considered incest with his mother no less evil than patricide, so he was embroiled in civil war before he had gathered much strength, driven from the throne and died. [J9]

Now this marriage between Thea Muse and her son Phraataces is a revealing event, for this incestuous royal relationship was not a Parthian custom, nor was it a Roman custom; the Romans even banned polygamy, let alone incest. However, incest was most definitely an old established Egyptian custom, and one that had been enthusiastically adopted by the Greco-Egyptian Ptolemaic dynasty. Nearly every Ptolemaic king and queen entered into an incestuous marriage of one kind or another, with Cleopatra VII's marriage to two of her younger brothers being a prime example. This evidence again suggests that Thea Muse was of Egyptian royal ancestry, and she was – through her mother Cleopatra VII. Strangely enough, this unpopular marriage between Thea Muse and Phraataces was mentioned by the biblical Jesus, as we shall see later, and this fact pulls this investigation ever closer towards its final conclusion.

Quite obviously, the attempt to force this incestual, Egyptian royal custom upon an unwilling Parthian court and population failed completely. Like Akhenaton before her, Thea Muse was reforming the traditions of the nation too far and too fast, and so the people rose up in revolt. The result was that within a couple of years Queen Thea Muse and her husband-son, King Phraataces, were exiled from Parthia. But where to? The information provided by Josephus is nonspecific, as he merely says that Phraataces was 'driven from the throne and died'. This sentence may initially make it appear that the exile was fatal, and that Phraataces died almost immediately; but that is not necessarily so, for Josephus is merely indicating that the king died in exile. In truth, Phraataces may have lived for many years before dying, while still remaining in exile.

The epitaph of Augustus Caesar inscribed upon the Ancyra Monument is only a little more illuminating when it records that:

> Kings of the Parthians, Tiridates, and later Phraates, the son of King Phraates, took refuge with me as suppliants. [12]

It is highly likely that 'Phraates, son of Phraates' was a reference to Phraataces, as that is what the latter name means; and so Augustus appears to be claiming that Phraataces 'took refuge' with him, presumably somewhere within the territories of the vast Roman Empire. The Cambridge History of Iran fleshes out this account with more detail when it indicates that:

> The new king (Phraataces) was driven from the throne in AD 4 and himself fled to Roman Syria, where he did not long survive. [13]

So the general opinion of historians is that Phraataces and Thea Muse ended up in Syria. But, apart from its close proximity to Parthia, why did the exiled royal couple choose Syria for their new residence? The answer to this question can probably be found in Josephus' *Antiquities* once more. Here, Josephus relates a story that Herod the Great's eastern border with Parthia was insecure. Since King Herod and King Phraates did not exactly see eye-to-eye, Herod was keen to settle some of his countrymen in Batanea, towards the east, to make this area more easy to defend.

Several locations are mentioned in the various texts, which lay to the east of Judaea and these are Gamala, Gaulanitis, Batanea and Trachonitis, and some of these locations will become important later in this research. Unfortunately, the precise geographical layout of many of these provinces and towns is unknown, but all of these areas lay to the east of the river Jordan and probably encompassed parts of what is now Jordan and Syria – between Amman and Damascus. Josephus says of this situation:

> Accordingly when (Herod) understood that there was a man that was a Jew was come out of Babylon, with five hundred horsemen, all of whom could shoot their arrows on horseback; and with a hundred of his relations, and had passed over the Euphrates and now abode at Antioch (in the north of the Levant opposite Cyprus). (Herod) sent for this man and promised to give him land in the area of Batanea ... he also promised to let him hold the country ... tax free. [J14]

Here we have a Jew from Babylon (Parthia) who was influential and powerful enough to own his own army, but nevertheless he was still evicted from Parthia and was forced to settle in lands to the east of the river Jordan that had been given to him by Herod. Given the modern political and theological map of Iraq (Babylon), which hardly seems very Jewish, this might sound like a fanciful tale; but in fact it is probably correct. The Jews had been (inadvertently) settled in Babylon by Nebuchadnezzar, who originally took them as captives. However, the Jewish community thrived in

Babylon and after they were set free by Cyrus the Great, many of them stayed on and became influential members of the Babylonian community, so it is not so unlikely that a Jew from across the Euphrates had a private army of 500 mounted archers.

In actual fact, the Jews of Iraq were a prominent feature of that country until the 1940s. However, the entire Arab world launched attacks against modern Israel in 1967 and 1973 (the Six Day and Yom Kippur wars), but were comprehensively beaten on both occasions by the Israelis. The result of these conflicts was the displacement of people throughout the region, with Palestinian exiles heading east and Iraqi Jews heading west. But while Israel accepted the Palestinian exiles back into the West Bank, the Iraqis refused to acknowledge the Jewish refugees; and in effect, the Iraqis had ethnically cleansed the entire Jewish population of Iraq. The Western press makes a great play on the plight of the displaced Palestinians, but for some reason ignores the Jewish refugees from the Arab lands of the Middle East.

It would seem that there were Jewish refugees from Babylon (Iraq) even at the turn of the first century AD, but who exactly was this 'influential Jew' with 500 mounted archers? Josephus says that his name was Zamaris, who had a son called Jachim and a grandson called Philip. Josephus is also saying that Zamaris and his men arrived in eastern Judaeo-Israel during the rule of Herod the Great, which would place this event in the years prior to 4 BC. Indeed the established date for Herod's annex of Trachonitis is about 25 BC.

This chronology would make it highly likely that this character called Zamaris was actually the Parthian prince called Tiridates, who temporarily became king of Parthia between 29 and 25 BC. Tiridates was, of course, thrown out of Parthia by Phraates IV, and so he would have been looking for lands to occupy during his exile. The account of Josephus would seem to be indicating that Tiridates fled to Antioch, but that Herod the Great gave him lands to the east of the Jordan to settle. The clue to Zamaris being one and the same as Tiridates is that Zamaris arrived in Judaeo-Syria with 500 mounted archers, and the name Tiridates means 'Great Archer' in Persian.

The only problem with this assertion is that it is unlikely that Tiridates, who was a Parthian prince, was a Jew. Having said this, the Jews were very influential in Parthia and it is known that a later king, Artabanus III, was crowned as king of Parthia by an influential Jew called Izates. In the circumstances, it is not so improbable that a Parthian prince had converted to Judaism.

It is also possible that Josephus' account has confused the exile of Prince Tiridates with the exile of Queen Thea Muse and King Phraataces.

Thea Muse was, of course, of Egyptian extract, and so she would have closely identified herself with the Judaism that was being practised in this era, as this early form of Judaism was distinctly Egyptian in its form, function and heritage. As the other books in this series have demonstrated, the Israelites were actually the Hyksos-Egyptians from Lower Egypt, and so their theology would have been distinctly Egyptian in nature. The biblical Book of Jeremiah makes this perfectly clear when it says that the Jews of the sixth century BC worshipped the Queen of Heaven, or the Queen of the Stars. [B15]

As we have already seen, the primary Queen of Heaven in Egypt was the goddess Isis, whose name was originally pronounced as Est or Ast . In later cultures and lands Isis became Astarte, Ishtar and Aphrodite. However, in the era of the biblical prophet Jeremiah, the Queen of Heaven who was most revered was the Queen of Sheba, whose name means the Queen of the Stars (Queen of Heaven) and who I have already identified as being Maachah Tamar II, the Egyptian daughter-wife of King David.

Even the monotheistic Judaism that we are more familiar with today was based upon the theology of the cult of Pharaoh Akhenaton, the 'heretic' pharaoh of the fourteenth century BC. I have already identified Akhenaton's brother, TuthMoses, as being the biblical Moses, which is why the hidden, singular deity of Akhenaton was called Aton and the hidden, singular Jewish god is sometimes called Adon.

So, in many respects Thea Muse's and Phraataces' Egyptian heritage could have identified them as being 'Jewish'; as many of the Jews of this era were similarly of Egyptian heritage. As the historian Strabo says of the people of Israel around the turn of the first century AD:

> This region lies towards the north; and it is inhabited ... by mixed stocks of people from Egyptian and Arabian and Phoenician tribes ... But though the inhabitants are mixed up thus, the most prevalent of the accredited reports in regard to the Temple at Jerusalem, represents the ancestors of the present Judaeans as Egyptians. [S16]

So the assertion that Zamaris was a Jew who fled from Babylon with 500 mounted archers could have been correct, for the flight of Queen Thea Muse Ourania and King Phraataces to Judaeo-Syria could have been interpreted in exactly this manner. The royal couple were certainly not of pure Parthian extract, and their incestuous marriage clearly marked them out as Egyptians [or Hyksos-Israelites]. More evidence for this will be given in later chapters. However, the fact that the Babylonians who settled in Batanea were most definitely something to do with Thea Muse and Phraataces can also be ascertained via a few pieces of interesting evidence.

Firstly, Thea Muse Ourania and Phraataces were the queen and king of Parthia. Although they had been exiled from that empire, they would undoubtedly have retained the support of some elements within the Parthian army. The primary armed forces in Parthia were the mounted archers, which is why the archer became a symbol of the nation. But the mention of a sizeable private army strongly suggests that this was a royal exile, and not the relocation of a disaffected baron. So if anyone could have left Babylon (Parthia) with 500 mounted archers and 100 relatives and officials – a sizeable retinue that does seem to be well in excess of the aspirations of any private individual – it would have been Queen Thea Muse and King Phraataces.

Secondly, there is the name of this Jewish exile who is supposed to have arrived with an army of mounted archers, which was Zamaris. The word *zamar* means 'bald' in both Hebrew and Persian. The Persian word *zamir* is quite explicit, referring to 'thin-haired', while the Hebrew version, *zamir* זמר, means 'prune', with close links to the concepts of 'woolly' and 'bristles'. In the circumstances, this is highly likely to have been an oblique reference to Julius Caesar, as the name Caesar means 'hair' in Latin and Julius was frequently ribbed about his receding hairline. While Prince Tiridates may have been linked to Augustus Caesar, who gave him sanctuary within the empire, the strongest link between a Caesar and a Parthian prince has to be between Julius Caesar and Phraataces. Given the new ancestry of Thea Muse being forged in these chapters, Phraataces would have been Julius' grandson and so Zamaris (the bald one) would have been an appropriate nickname, even though Phraataces himself was not in any way bald.

Thirdly, the most compelling piece of evidence – to prove that Thea Muse Ourania settled in this province called Batanea, to the east of the river Jordan – is that the alternative name for this region was Auranitis (Hauranitis). Indeed, the area is still known as the Hauran. Modern text books will say that the name Auranitis (Aurania) was derived from the Hebrew word *khavran* חורן meaning 'hollow' or 'cave'; however, this just has to be a convenient error as it does not even sound correct. The proper derivation is from the Hebrew *haran* הרן, which became the Greek *oranos* ορεινος, with both words meaning 'mountain'. However, it was from the sacred 'mountains' of Egypt, the pyramids, that an association between mountains and heavens was derived – an association that gave rise to the age-old adage 'as above, so below'. This argument is reinforced by the interpretation of John Lightfoot, the venerable seventeenth century theologian who said that:

> Mount Hauran (not the region called Hauran) is reckoned up amongst those

> hills, at the top of which, by lifting up some flaming torches, the Jews were wont to give notice of the new year. [17] (Author's brackets.)

Although Lightfoot would not be aware of the deeper meaning of this celebration, since the Hyksos-Israelites were descended from Egypt, the original 'mountains' that were used in this ritual were located at Giza. The pyramids were the man-made mountains that reached out to the heavens, and the Great Pyramid [Mt Sinai] with its platform on its summit, may even have been the greatest astronomical observatory of the ancient world; from which torches could indeed be waved. It was through this symbolism that *oranos* ορεινος, meaning 'mountain', became *ouranos* or *auranos* ουρανος meaning 'heaven'. So the lands to the east of the river Jordan were not named after a boring cave, but after the great, imperishable celestial heavens. In fact, to be more precise, the lands of Aurania (Auranitis) were not named after the heavens themselves, they were actually named after the queen who took up residence in this very location: Queen Thea Muse Aurania (Ourania), whose name could be interpreted as meaning 'the Queen of Heaven'.

Fig 18. Painting adorning the Gornji Grad cathedral in Slovenia, which demonstrates how pyramid iconography can be covertly introduced into orthodox Christianity. See the book 'Jesus' for further examples.

Josephus' report about an exiled Parthian Jew, who fled to Judaeo-Syria with 500 mounted archers and 100 of his own family and courtiers, may well have been a reference to the exile of Queen Thea Muse Ourania and King Phraataces. That this extract was placed in the chapters in Josephus' *Antiquities* that deal with Herod the Great's reign may have been due to the fact that it was Herod Philip, the son of Herod the Great and the tetrarch of Syria, who subsequently ruled these very same lands to the east of the river Jordan. In other words, the exile of Zamaris probably occurred in AD 4 instead of 25 BC, and it was actually Herod the tetrarch (Herod Philip) who welcomed these exiles into the lands to the east of the river Jordan that became known as Batanea or Aurania (Auranitis). (The flight of a Prince Tiridates from Parthia to Syria in 25 BC may have be mistaken with the flight of another, better-known Prince Tiridates from Parthia to Syria in AD 36.)

If Zamaris' exile was in AD 4, then we now have a good idea of exactly where Thea Muse and Phraataces would have fled to. Herod Philip, being the ruler of the lands of modern Syria and Jordan, required a friendly military force to secure his eastern borders with Parthia, and who better to perform this task than an exiled Parthian prince (or king) who had just strolled into his realm with 500 mounted archers. The offer of lands free of tax to this royal exile would have been a small price to pay, considering the security they could offer to the eastern borders of Herod Philip's realm. The subsequent history of this region will fully support this assertion, as we shall see shortly.

Umm el-Jimal

Where exactly in the province of Batanea or Aurania did Thea Muse locate her new capital city? What we are looking for here is a new city that was founded in the first century AD; and bearing in mind the illustrious Egypto-Parthian ancestry of Thea Muse, perhaps we are also looking for a city that tried to reflect the former royal grandeur that she was used to. There is one such site in the Kingdom of Aurania, modern Hauran, and that is the long abandoned city of Umm el-Jimal, which is situated out on the vast rolling plains that lie to the east of modern Amman:

> Although it was continuously occupied for 800 years from the first century BC to the eighth century AD and again from World War I to the present, Umm el-Jimal shows no evidence of occupation before the first century, and it lay completely abandoned between AD 750 and the 20th century. [18]

The pottery stratigraphy of the site was quite conclusive in this respect.

Although early Roman pottery was found, it was all mixed with middle Roman pottery and so the earliest date for the settlement of this site would appear to be the turn of the first century AD. These dates should place this fine city, once home to some 5,000 or more inhabitants, well within the sphere of influence of the Nabataean kingdom, which resided just to the south of Aurania at Petra, and it is the Nabataeans who are regarded as the prime candidates for the founding of this city. However, the archaeology of the site simply fails to confirm this. Professor De Vries says of this lack of evidence:

> Consider this archaeological puzzle: the distinctive Nabataean pottery, so common at southern sites, is almost totally lacking at otherwise identifiable Nabataean sites such as Umm el-Jimal. [19]

If these people at Umm el-Jimal were not Nabataean, then where did they come from? There are many inscriptions on the site, which are mostly written in Greek, with only a few in Nabataean and one or two in Arabic. This may seem to count against an association with Thea Muse and Phraataces and their Egypto-Parthian exiles; but of course Thea Muse herself was the daughter of Cleopatra IV, who was a Ptolemaic queen whose first language was Greek. Furthermore, the Seleucid dynasties of Persia (Parthia) were also Greek, and no doubt many of the courtiers in Parthia still spoke Greek. This preference can be seen in the coins of Parthia, including those of Thea Muse and Phraataces, which have Greek inscriptions. This preference for the Greek language lasted right through the Arsacid dynasty, but later coins demonstrate that the Greek language was being lost, as the inscriptions are only of garbled Greek letters.

Greek had also become the common language of Israelo-Syria, which is why the New Testament accounts were all written in Greek and the lands around Galilee to the west of Aurania were regarded as completely Hellenistic. However, while the predominant language of this area and of Umm el-Jimal in particular was definitely Greek, the names given in these inscriptions demonstrate that many of these people must have had Arabic or Aramaic origins. Despite this hint of a Greek-speaking Arabic (Parthian) heritage, the exact ancestry of this new town in Aurania remains elusive. Again, Professor De Vries says of this conundrum:

> Granted that the inhabitants were indigenous to the general area, we still ask, "Where did they come from?" and "Why did they settle here?" It is probable that they were simply nomads of the region attracted to a more sedentary life by the new stability of Roman order, perhaps even encouraged by the Roman authorities in the same way that modern Bedouin have been by the Jordanian Government. [22]

As we have already seen, the most likely explanation for the settlement of Umm el-Jimal is given in Josephus' *Antiquities*, where he clearly states that a man called Zamaris had fled from Parthia with 500 mounted archers and 100 close relations and courtiers. Herod the tetrarch (probably Herod Philip) had settled these refugees in Batanea, a location which we now know was almost identical to Auranitis (Aurania), in order to secure his eastern borders with Parthia. The archaeologists who have worked at Umm el-Jimal have recognised the strategic importance of the site, and they indicate that el-Jimal:

> ... fits well with the Roman development of a fortified frontier from Aqaba to the Euphrates, the Limes Arabicus, as a defense line against threats of nomadic raiding and Persian invasion. [23]

That Umm el-Jimal was a strategic frontier city is borne out by its extensive fortifications, and no doubt this city did indeed serve as a salient city that supplied the other smaller fortifications in the surrounding region. But this was not strictly speaking a Roman defensive system, it was actually Judaic, with the kings and regional commanders of the region being the Herod tetrarchs (Herod Archelous and Herod Philip). Although it has to be said that both Herod tetrarchs and their father Herod the Great were given control over these lands by Rome, and it was Rome who oversaw and occasionally underpinned the tetrarch's troop movements in the area and the wider political strategy of her eastern borders.

The ruins of Umm el-Jimal that are visible today are actually the remains of the Byzantine town that was built several centuries after the original settlement. In fact, it would appear that the location of the city moved by a few hundred meters, and the ruins of the old town were stripped away and reused in the new. The fact that many tombstones were reused as building material in the new Byzantine city may also point towards these new settlers being of different cultural origins, for they had no respect for the dead of the old town.

The exact nature of the old town is not fully understood as it is much ruined, however this was no mud-brick or wattle-and-daub village for rustics:

> ... the architecture is less elaborate than in the Byzantine town, but the place is extremely rich in high quality pottery, including much imported wares such as *terra siggilata*. The new balloon photographs reveal the intriguing possibility that the settlement may have been planned with a rectangular layout. [24]

The fact that the new inhabitants of this area had the resources to build an entire new city out of stone, while simultaneously importing luxury goods from the Roman empire, would suggest great wealth – the kind of wealth that an exiled royal family might have been able to take with them on their recent flight from Parthia. Also, the fact that these imported goods all appear to be Roman, while Parthia lay on the province's doorstep, would suggest that the town did not have trading relations with Parthia. Indeed, if this town was conceived, constructed and inhabited by Thea Muse and her fellow exiles from Parthia, this would not be so surprising.

: drawn by Bert de Vries.

Fig 19. Map of the city of Umm el-Jimal in Aurania (modern Hauran) – the Mother of Egypt and birthplace of the biblical Jesus.

The ruins that remain at the site today are extensive and while they are not so ornate and decorative as the Roman city in nearby Jerash, the ruins suggest that both the old and the new cities were well constructed and relatively luxurious. There are several enormous water storage cisterns that would have provided generous supplies of water during the long, dry summers, while many of the houses appear to have been three or four storeys high; the latter feature being similar to the high-rise apartments constructed in Saba, in modern Yemen.

The livestock of the Jimalians were also well provided for, with accommodation being constructed for the flocks and herds within each house. This would again indicate that the Jimalians had a siege mentality of the inhabitants of a border-fortress city, for even their livestock had to be corralled within the city walls. The following description of these animal pens and stalls may be of importance in later chapters:

> In most cases, a large portion of the bottom floor (of each building) was used to house animals. There are rooms with well-constructed mangers, often with tethering devices for large animals (donkeys, horses, cows), and bigger rooms for the simple indoor penning of smaller animals (sheep, goats). [25]

The origins of the name of Umm el-Jimal remains a mystery, and Professor Howard Butler, who did much of the early archaeology of this site, says of the name for this town:

> This ancient ruined city has long been called by the Arabs Umm idj-Djimal (Umm el-Jimal), which, being translated, is 'Mother of Camels'.... It is not definitely known what the city was called in Roman or early Christian times; but 'Mother of Camels' it is now, and no name could fit it better, especially in the spring time when the Bedouin, with hundreds of breeding camels, pitch their tents around the walls of the city. [26]

As Professor De Vries points out, the name of a town is an important element, because unless its name is known it cannot be placed within the historical record with any certainty. Was it the town of Surattha from Ptolemy's *Geography?* Or was it perhaps the town of Thainatha from the *Notitia Dignitatum?* The truth is that, despite Umm el-Jimal being quite a substantial settlement, nobody knows what it was originally called, although it is known that the present name goes back at least to the early nineteenth century.

So, Umm el-Jimal currently remains aloof from the historical record because its original name is unknown. Or is it? What if the Arabic name for the town *is* the original? What if it may be linked to the biblical town of

Gamala? This possibility has been largely discounted because the name does not entirely fit the location. 'Mother of Camels' might suggest a Bedouin trading post or a center of some caravan route, which Umm el-Jimal was not (originally). Rather, the town was a strategic frontier post, a local military supply center, and in the later Byzantine era it became a devout Christian city, containing no less than fifteen Christian churches. So why then, apart from the odd nomadic traders on their camels passing by, was the town called Jimal, meaning 'camel'?

The answer probably lies in the Egyptian interpretation of this word, for the Arabic word for camel was probably derived from the Egyptian original, which was *kamar (kamal)* . However, this Egyptian word for a camel had another meaning, and that was Kam  which referred to the country of Egypt itself. In other words, an alternative rendering for Umm el-Jimal might well be 'Mother of Egypt'. Cleopatra VII was known as the Isis of Egypt, and since Isis was the mother of all living things, then it is likely that Cleopatra was also known as the Mother of Egypt. The possibility exists, therefore, that Cleopatra's daughter, Thea Muse Ourania, inherited this title and used it for the new town she founded in exile. And so the town of Umm el-Jimal in Aurania was actually the town of Umm el-Kam(el) in Ourania – the Mother of Egypt in the Kingdom of Thea Muse Ourania.

Julia

Finally, there is the interesting case of the name for one of the Byzantine churches in Umm el-Jimal. Now these churches were built many centuries after Thea Muse and should have had nothing directly to do with these events, except that one of the inscriptions on a window lintel was rather older than it was first thought to be:

> In 1956 G Corbett did an architectural study of the 'Julianos' Church in order to test Butler's conclusion that this church had been built in AD 344. Corbett concluded that the Julianos Inscription from which the date was derived was actually a funerary inscription reused secondarily in the building. [27]

So an old tombstone had been reused in the construction of a later Byzantine church, and this tombstone was dedicated to someone called Julianos, a Greek rendering of the Latin Julia. It may or may not be coincidental, but the daughter of Thea Muse was called Julia Ourania. Has the tombstone of Thea Muse's daughter been discovered in Umm el-Jimal?

Fig 20. The Julianos inscription at Umm el-Jimal.

IV

Fourth Sect of Judaism

The next important character of note in this region and era springs, once more, from the lands to the east of the river Jordan. His name is given as Judas the Gaulonite, who came to prominence at about the time of the Jewish taxation under the Roman consul Cyrenius (Quirinius), in about AD 6. This is the taxation event that is mentioned in the biblical account of the birth of Jesus:

> And it came to pass in those days, that there went out a decree from Caesar Augustus, that all the world should be taxed. (And this taxing was first made when Cyrenius was governor of Syria.) And all went to be taxed, every one into his own city. And Joseph also went up from Galilee ... to be taxed with Mary his espoused wife, being great with child. And so it was, that, while they were there, the days were accomplished that she should be delivered. [B1]

Note here that the governor in charge of the taxation was Cyrenius, who was based in Syria, not Judaea. This may be an important point in the arguments to come. So it was during this taxation census that the biblical Jesus was said to have been born, or in other words, Jesus was born in AD 6. This verse does, of course, greatly conflict with the accounts that say that Jesus was threatened by King Herod the Great, and his reported murder of all the infants in Bethlehem; an event which, if it ever occurred, would place the birth of Jesus just prior to 4 BC.

This topic has been widely debated in my and other works and so I don't propose to go into great detail here. Suffice it to say that Herod the Great did murder a number of children because of a dispute over the royal succession, but these were all his own. The fact that Jesus is said to have been threatened by this royal infanticide again demonstrates that he was of royal blood.

Having said this, it is more likely that Jesus was born during the great taxation under Cyrenius, and so we need to account for this error. The differing birth dates being given in the biblical account may be due to many reasons, but one possibility is that, since Jesus had brothers, this may be a record of two sons being born to Mary: one in 4 BC, the other in AD 6. Alternatively, the account in Matthew about Herod killing the children may be referring to Herod Archelous, the son of King Herod the Great, who was Tetrarch (king) of Judaea from 4 BC to AD 6. As this rather short reign-length suggests, Archelous was quickly deposed for being as much of a tyrant as his father was in his later years, so this confusion between the tyrannical Herod Archelous and the equally tyrannical Herod the Great is always possible.

This new character in our saga, Judas, came to power during this great taxation under Cyrenius and he was known as the Gaulonite; that is, someone from the Golan Heights that lay to the east of the Sea of Galilee. In other words, Judas was from almost exactly the same area as the exiled Prince Zamaris from Parthia, who had settled his people to the east of the Jordan in Batanea, or Auranitis (Aurania). That there is a link between these two characters is implied by their common concerns. It was stressed by Josephus Flavius that Prince Zamaris was given the lands of Batanea tax free, in order to protect Herod's eastern borders from attacks by the Parthians. Yet Judas the Gaulonite (or Judas of Gamala) came to power as part of a powerful Jewish faction who were fighting the new Roman taxation by Cyrenius.

> Judas, a Gaulonite of the city of Gamala ... became zealous to draw the people to revolt, who both said that this taxation was no better than an introduction to slavery, and exhorted the nation to assert their liberty. [J2]

In other words, both Zamaris and Judas arose from the same region and both had the same political concerns: taxation and independence, both from Jerusalem and from Rome. In addition, this same Judas was also said to be a Galilean from the city of Gamala, which is interesting as Galilee and Gamala are on opposite banks of the Jordan and are therefore not entirely compatible with each other.

So was Judas simply a nickname for Zamaris? Well, Ioudas (Judas) Ιουδας is simply a Greek rendering of the Hebrew word for a Jew. Since Zamaris was pointedly said to have been a Jew, and an exotic Babylonian Jew no less, then he may well have been called 'the Jew' as a common nickname. So yes, this Judas of Gamala (Judas the Gaulonite) may well have simply been another name for Zamaris – the Babylonian Jew who arrived in Judaeo-Syria with 500 mounted archers and 100 relatives and courtiers, and who may have founded the city in Batanea called Umm el-Jimal. While this is all a little speculative at present, there is another reference to Judas of Gamala in the Acts of the Apostles that sheds some more light on the matter:

> Then stood there up one in the council, a Pharisee, named Gamaliel, a doctor of the law, had in reputation among all the people, and commanded to put the apostles forth a little leniency ... For before these days rose up Theudas, boasting himself to be somebody; to whom a number of men, about four hundred, joined themselves: who was slain; and all, as many as obeyed him, were scattered, and brought to nought. After this man rose up Judas of Galilee (Gamala) in the days of the taxing, and drew away much people after him: he also perished; and all, even as many as obeyed him, were dispersed. [B3]

This indicates that before Judas there was another revolutionary called Theudas Θευδας. But, as the theologian Adam Clarke acknowledges, Theudas is probably a corruption of the name Judas. So here we have two similar characters, possibly a father and son, both of whom were revolutionaries and both were known as being prominent Jews from Gamala. Note that the man defending the disciples was a man called Gamaliel; a name derived from the root *gamal* meaning 'camel', as is the city of Gamala. In the circumstances, this 'name' has to be a reference to an important person from Gamala, for the text is talking about Judas of Gamala. This Pharisee called Gamaliel may have been Zamaris' compatriot, Zadok the Pharisee. The obvious link here between the city of Gamala and the city of Umm el-Jimal (Gamal) will be explored later.

The point of this particular investigation is that this would seem to be the same Judas of Gamala who is mentioned later as being the leader of the 'fourth sect' of Judaism, and who is likely to have been from Babylon (Parthia). If so, it would seem that there were three generations of revolutionaries, who were known as Zamaris, Jacim and Philip (by Josephus Flavius) or Theudas and Judas (according to the author of Acts), who were important religious leaders of a new sect of Judaism, and who were living in Gamala, a city that resided in Batanea (or Aurania). The fact that these people were said by Josephus to be Babylonians, strongly links them with the Parthian exiles of Thea Muse. However, the fact that these religious revolutionaries lived in Batanea also strongly links them with the gospel accounts, as we shall see shortly.

This confusion of locations is not exactly a minor point, to be glossed over as a scribe's transcription error of no importance. Here is a family that may well link the Parthian exiles of Thea Muse with the family of Jesus, and so what we now need is a reference to the biblical Jesus that places him in the same context; one that demonstrates that he too was related in some fashion to the town of Gamala. Strange as it may seem, there was a later character who was given the exact same title as Judas of Gamala, but this character was much better known – for this revolutionary from Gamala was indeed called Jesus. As I have pointed out in the book *Jesus*, there were several Jesuses mentioned in the works of Josephus Flavius, one of whom was called Jesus of Gamala and another who was called Jesus of Sapphias:* the governor of Tiberias who came from Galilee.

However, upon further research, I have already demonstrated that these two Jesuses were actually the same person, and in addition they also seem to be inextricably linked to the biblical Jesus. Thus we have a situation where Judas the Gaulonite was from Gamala and Galilee while the biblical Jesus was also from Gamala and Galilee. But these two characters were not the same individual, as this Judas came to power in about AD 6 and the biblical Jesus was not at his peak of influence until about AD 60. (The book *Jesus* explains this later date, rather than the orthodox AD 30.)

There is the possibility, however, that these two characters – Judas of Gamala and Galilee [Zamaris] and Jesus of Gamala and Galilee [Jesus] were related; perhaps even father and son. Evidence for this can be seen in the name of Zamaris' son, who was called Jacim. The name Jacim is derived from the Greek *jacin* υακιν meaning 'sapphire', and in a similar fashion I have already identified the biblical Jesus with Josephus Flavius' character who was called Jesus of Sapphias. Thus the son of Zamaris appears to have had the same name as Jesus himself, and so Jesus of Sapphias may have referred to 'Jesus whose mother was called Sapphias (Sapphira)'. The reference to a sapphire may well relate to Jesus mother, Mary, who is always identified with the colour blue, as we shall see.

Likewise, the reference to Galilee may not be exactly what it seems either. Just as the biblical authorities like to persuade us that Jesus came from Nazareth, when that town did not exist in that era, they also like to imply that Jesus came from Galilee. But the strange linking of Judas the Galilean, who was nevertheless from across the river Jordan in Gamala, strongly suggests that the term Galilee did not refer to a location; for Gamala

* I had previously thought that the term Sapphias was derived from the city of Sepphoris in Galillee. However, Sapphira Σαπφειρη was the wife of Ananias and this couple were mentioned directly before the character called Judas of Gamala in Acts 5:37. Since Ananias was simply a priestly title, Judas and Ananias may have been one and the same, and thus this Jesus was probably the son of Sapphira (the blue lady) and Ananias.

and Galilee were miles apart. But if Galilee was not a reference to the Sea of Galilee, then what did it mean? Well, in actual fact, the name Galilee is actually taken from the Greek *galilaia* γαλιλαια, which means 'circle'.

Therefore, there are two alternatives for the true meaning of *galilee* in this context. Firstly, it may simply refer to a revolutionary or a fanatic. Note that exactly the same term is given today to a person or society that upsets the social apple-cart. A revolution tends to turn a society completely around, and so the proletariat become the leaders and the leaders become the proletariat. In other words, a revolution makes society revolve in a circle, or in a *galilee*. Thus the title 'Jesus the Galilean' may simply refer to 'Jesus the Revolutionary', the Che Guevara of first century Judaeo-Israel.

Alternatively, having written so much about the circling rituals of the Hyksos-Israelite people, it is also possible that this term refers to this circling ritual. This ritual is still performed today, of course, but it is now to be found in the Al-Haram mosque at Mecca rather than in Israel or Egypt. That both Judas of Gamala and Jesus of Gamala may have been involved in these same circling rituals further strengthens the links between the two characters. Also, the fact that these circling rituals survived more openly in the lands of Parthia, rather than in the Judaeo-Christian West, likewise strengthens their links to Parthia.

However, the circling rituals did not die out completely in the West, for circling is also a central part of masonic ritual, where it is known as the 'first point' or the god principle. This is the reason for early Templar churches being circular – as was the Christian cathedral of Aya Sophia in Istanbul and the later Templar church in the Inner Temple of London – so that circular perambulations of the church could take place. In masonic ritual, however, it is made rather more obvious that this circling ritual is intended to represent the circuit of the Sun, planets and stars.

It is probably just one of those quirks of coincidence that the great sixteenth century astronomer, Galileo Galilei was named after the circling motion of the moons and planets that he eventually studied. (His father was a mathematician, which may explain the coincidence.)

Bethany

If these two influential characters, Zamaris and Jesus, were related, then this does infer that the biblical Jesus came from the same location as the exiled Thea Muse and Phraataces. It would appear that all of these characters were from Gamala and the lands to the east of the Jordan – in other words, they were from Batanea or Auranitis (Aurania, the modern Hauran). While this assertion may still seem speculative at present,

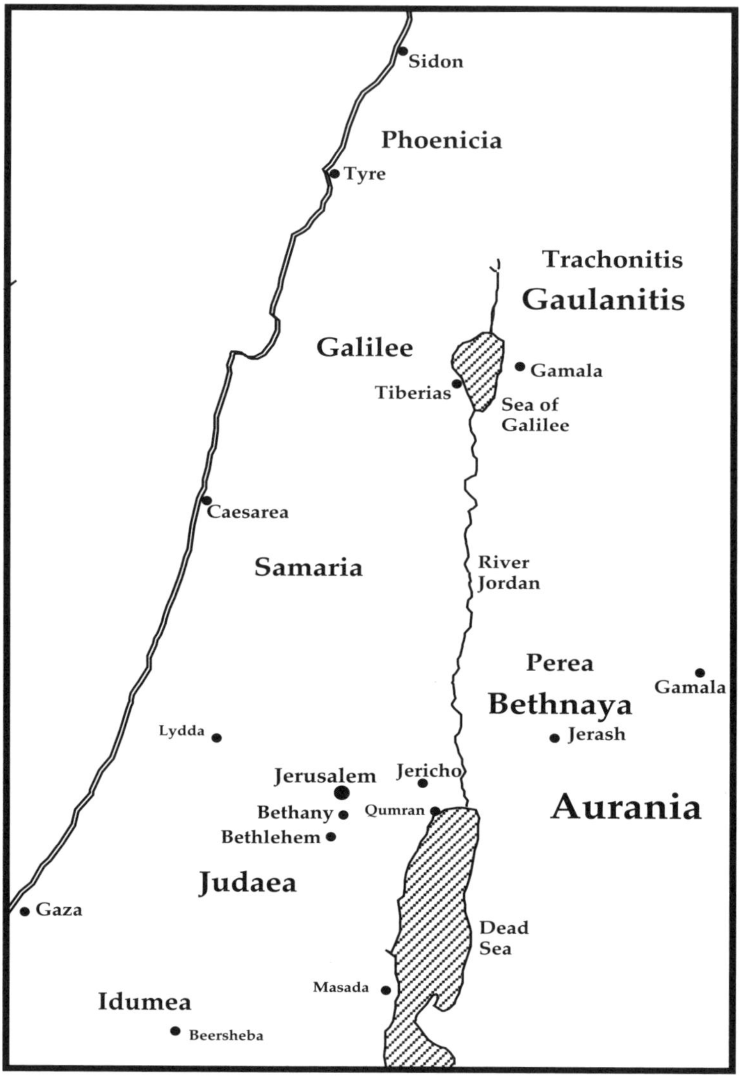

Fig 24. Map of first century Syrio-Judaea.

especially in regard to the biblical Jesus, the evidence for this claim is to be found once more in the Gospels:

> And being in Bethany in the house of Simon the leper, as he (Jesus) sat among them, there came a woman having an alabaster box of ointment of spikenard very precious; and she brake the box, and poured it on his head. [B4]

As ever with these biblical verses, one needs to understand the background to the story before the correct translation can be made. In this case, the term 'leper' does not refer to a disease, but rather to a religious sect. Simon was actually called *lepros* λεπρος meaning 'scaly', and this is actually a covert reference to a fish – the sign of the later Christian sect. In fact, since the term Nazarene has much the same meaning in Arabic, Simon the 'leper' was just being called the Nazarene here, the same as Jesus was. See the book *Jesus* for more details on this fish symbolism and its connection with the zodiac.

More importantly, however, the woman with the alabaster jar in this verse was, of course, Mary Magdalene. But Mary has already been shown in many works to have been the wife of Jesus and, in addition, I have also demonstrated that Mary was the sister-wife of Jesus. While this may have seemed like a fanciful marital union when I penned this hypothesis many years ago in the book *Jesus*, the links that are being demonstrated here between Thea Muse and the biblical family make this incestuous union a near certainty. Clearly, Thea Muse and Phraataces were adhering to the Egyptian rules of consanguinity, when the mother married her son; and so for this particular royal family, the marriage between Jesus and his sister Mary would have been a perfectly normal (even mandatory) event.

What this sibling marriages does, however, is to strengthen the links between Jesus and this favourite house at Bethany, which was owned by Simon the Leper [Simon the Nazarene]. It is clear that Mary and Martha lived at this house in Bethany and it is also clear that this important but shadowy character called Mary of Bethany was, in fact, Mary Magdalene. It is already obvious from the many biblical citations that this house at Bethany was a favourite place for Jesus and his disciples to stay; but if Mary Magdalene was Jesus' sister then the house at Bethany probably belonged to Jesus' and Mary's brother, Simon.

In short, it would seem that Jesus and Mary Magdalene came from Bethany, and yet the lands that were given to the exiled Parthians (Queen Thea Muse and King Phraataces-Zamaris) were known as Batanea. However, it would only take a simple consonant change from a 't' to a 'th' for Batanea to become Bethanya, or Bethany. Thus Mary of Bethany was not from a Bethany that lay close to Jerusalem, but from Bethanya, the province which had been created and settled by the exiled Parthians. Incidentally, it is likely that Bethanya was the name of an administrative region encompassing all of Gamala, Gaulanitis and Trachonitis, and so it was relatively large in extent.

The classical biblical town of Bethany is said to have been located just outside Jerusalem on the road to Jericho, which is why I have previously said that this was Mary's (and Jesus') Jerusalem residence, within easy commuting distance of the city. But if Jesus was from Gamala, then this house near Jerusalem was a long way from home and a little out of place in the biblical texts. The possibility that Bethany referred instead to Bethanya would clear up this confusion in an instant, for Gamala was a major town in the province of Bethanya. The fact that it was this eastern Bethany that was intended by the gospels, and not the location near Jerusalem, is confirmed to us by the accounts relating to John the Baptist. It is said of John that:

> These things were done in Bethany Βηθανια beyond the Jordan, where John was baptising. [B5]

Readers with a King James Bible will find that this town has been translated as Bethabara βηθαβαρα, meaning 'the crossing over the Jordan'. However, it has been established by theologians that, of all the ancient versions of the Bible that are still extant, the vast majority use the name Bethany instead of Bethabara. This slip of the pen in one or two versions of the New Testament would have been convenient, had it not been spotted and corrected in time (in a more enlightened era); for the incorrect name of Bethabara keeps the biblical events close to Jerusalem and away from their true location to the east of the river Jordan.

Having sorted out this little error, it would seem the true import of the gospels is that John the Baptist was resident at this Bethany (alias Bethanya or Aurania) to the east of the river Jordan – which is why there is a modern tourist trap just east of the river Jordan that claims to be the place of Jesus' baptism. However, this lucrative tourist trap fails to understand that Bethanya was an administrative region, not a specific location or town, and so this location conveniently close to the Jordan is unlikely to be the historical location for the baptism of Jesus. In fact, since the city of Umm el-Jimal contains a number of cisterns, one of which is so large that it looks very much like an Egyptian ritual bathing pool, the baptism of Jesus could have taken place many miles from the river Jordan.

Since Jesus was baptised in this region called Bethanya, it is this region and not the Bethany near Jerusalem that has to be central to the New Testament story. Thus, in one swift stroke of a correction marker, many of the New Testament accounts and stories have been wrenched eastwards, away from Jerusalem and towards the east. In fact, so far eastwards have they travelled, that all of the stories about Mary, Martha and Lazarus are likely to have occurred to the east of the river Jordan in Bethanya (Aurania).

The biblical Concordance has assumed that this location called Bethany was the name of a town. But since it was located to the east of the Jordan, in the province of Bethanya, it could simply have been a reference to the whole province rather than a town. Indeed, since Bethany was supposed to be one of the largest towns in this province, both John and Mary may well have been resident in the town of Gamala, which resided in the province of Bethanya (Bethany). So Mary of Bethany may have been Mary of Gamala. Since we have just seen that the biblical Jesus was sometimes called Jesus of Gamala, and he was also the brother-husband of Mary, this would make a great deal of sense.

When I wrote the book *Jesus*, I did wonder for a long time why I had ended up with a brother (Jesus) whose family home was in Gamala and his sister (Mary Magdalene) whose family home was near Jerusalem. This was simply one of many loose ends that I was unable to clear up at the time, but the rest of the underlying analysis was so convincing that it had to be based on a historical truth. Now, in the light of further research and revelations, it would seem that this separation was not an issue at all, for the location called Bethany has now taken a giant leap across to Syrio-Judaea and into Bethanya or Aurania, the province in which the city of Gamala resided.

That the true home of Jesus and his family should be relocated out onto the plains of Aurania, the modern Hauran to the east of the city of Amman, is reinforced by the Tarmida,* one of the holy books of the Mandaeans, the secretive sect of proto-Christians who now inhabit the marshlands of Iraq (the Marsh Arabs). This rather secretive work is known, by its colophons, to date from the Parthian period; and it begins its narrative just before the life of Jesus. Its opening passages say:

> The interior of the Harran (ie Hauran) admitted them, that city which has Nasurai in it, so that there should not be a road (passage?) for the kings of the Chaldeans (Parthians). [6]

Here, in the first sections of the Tarmida, seems to be an accurate description of the precise situation I have proposed for the city of Umm el-Jimal. The interior of the Hauran (Aurania or Haurania) is where Umm el-Jimal is located, and its function was indeed to act as a frontier town and prevent the passage of the Parthian army into Syria and Judaea. But it would seem that within this city were the Nasurai people, which just has to be a corruption of the Arabic term 'Nasrani' meaning 'Christian'. The term 'Nasurai' was also an early name for the Mandaeans, and since the Mandaeans are vaguely a Christian sect who appear to venerate John the Baptist and regard Jesus as a false prophet (an accusation that we have already seen was rife in the first century AD), the term Nasurai must refer to an early form of 'Christianity'. Now while it may be claimed that a sect that denies the divinity of Jesus cannot be Christian in the true sense of the word, the Knights Templar were

* Was the name for the Tarmida derived from the Judaic Talmud?

also reputed to have followed a version of the Mandaean creed, and this belief system formed a part of the reasoning for the Catholic witch-hunt against them. Although their beliefs may not have been wholly orthodox, the Templars would still have considered themselves to be 'Christian'.

As far as the import of this quote is concerned, while we know that the city of Umm el-Jimal was definitely a Christian city during the Byzantine era, as it contains sixteen Byzantine Christian churches, this passage in the Mandaean's holy book comes immediately before the birth of Jesus. If the Mandaean chronology is correct, then they are indicating that the early Christians came from Umm el-Jimal, just as I have suspected. Since Umm el-Jimal lies within Aurania, or the province of Thea Muse Ourania (Aurania), this also links the biblical story with Thea Muse and Phraataces.

Later passages in the Tarmida indicate that the Nasurai (the early Mandaean 'Christians') were very close to the biblical family, as the Nasurai were persecuted along with Jesus' disciples. These passages also claim that some of the ancestors and rituals of the Mandaeans came from Egypt, which would make sense in terms of Thea Muse being an Egyptian princess. However, the evidence then gets even more intriguing, for the texts go on to identify the Nasurai with the Parthians!

> The importance of this document (the Tarmida) lies in the implication that the Nasurai are identical with the Parthians, since the latter correspond with the Ardban Malka (the king of the Nasurai). [7]

Now this is very interesting, for the Nasurai (an early Christian sect) are being described as being Parthian; and their king is said to be Ardban, who we can confidently identify as Artabanus II of Parthia, who ruled from about AD 10 to AD 38. So, this document appears to claim that many of the early Christians were also Parthians, and yet this would only make sense if the biblical family were descended from Thea Muse, as has been proposed. But why, in this case, was the king of the Nasurai identified with Artabanus and not Jesus?

The answer to this question has to be that there were at least three waves of Parthian exiles into Syrio-Judaea – ranging from King Tiridates and King Phraataces to King Vonones I, the prince who Augustus set upon the throne of Parthia after Thea Muse and Phraataces were exiled – and not all of these exiles from Parthia believed that Jesus was a rightful Parthian prince. We know that this is true of the Nasurai (the Mandaeans), for they venerated John the Baptist as a great prophet, whatever his ancestry may have been, but not Jesus, who was regarded as the Egyptian False Prophet. Quite obviously, Thea Muse Ourania and Phraataces were having an uphill struggle to convince everyone, even from among their own exiled community, that their

Fig 25. The mountain-top citadel of Gamala.

descendants should be the rightful claimants to the throne – a point that the New Testament also makes clear.

Nevertheless, the evidence from these secretive Mandaean texts clearly supports the argument that the early Christians were related to the Parthians, and these texts also support the notion that the original location for these early Christians was the city of Umm el-Jimal in the Hauran (Aurania or Bethanya, the province of Thea Muse Ourania).

Gamala

There is one other point that needs to be cleared up, in regard to the original location for the family of Jesus, and that is the precise location of the biblical town of Gamala; the town that both Judas and Jesus appear to have been most closely connected with. It would seem that Gamala was named after the Hebrew *gamal* גמל meaning 'camel'; and so, just like the frontier town of Umm el-Jimal (Gamal) that was discussed extensively in the last chapter, the biblical town of Gamala was also named after a camel [or Egypt]. So was Gamala the same town as Umm el-Jimal?

Unfortunately for this idea, Josephus Flavius gives us a very good description of Gamala, and the great siege of the town by the Romans in AD 67. Gamala is said to have been a mountain-top refuge to the east of the Sea of Galilee, an invincible Masada of the north. Just such a fortress was recently discovered and excavated by Israeli archaeologists, and this fortress does, indeed, appear to have been Josephus' citadel of Gamala. It even comes complete with a breach in the defensive wall and piles of used Roman *balista* stones, just as Josephus recounts:

> The remains of the city are located on a rocky basalt ridge surrounded by deep gorges, with a shallow saddle separating it from the rest of the ridge,

> providing the city with outstanding defensive advantages. The top of the hill is narrow and pointed, creating a very steep slope in the north; the city was built on the more graduated southern slope. [J8]

The geography of this mountain citadel fits Josephus' description of Gamala like a glove, and the reason it was called Gamala is because it was built upon two hilltops – like the paired humps of a Bactrian camel. However, it is always possible that there were two Gamalas (as, indeed, there are to this day), because although this Gamala to the east of the Sea of Galilee is a fine location for a citadel, it is a truly terrible location for 500 mounted archers. In another section, Josephus says of Gamala:

> King Herod Agrippa* also bid Philip to take some horsemen with him, and to go quickly to the citadel of Gamala, and to bring out thence all his domestics, and to restore the Babylonians to Batanea again. He also gave it him in charge to take all possible care that none of his subjects should be guilty of making any innovation. Accordingly, upon these directions from the king, he made haste to do what he was commanded. [J9]

Now this Philip was the son of Jacim and the grandson of Zamaris, the Babylonian Jew who fled to Syrio-Judaea with 500 mounted archers and who settled his people in Batanea (Bethanya or Aurania). Note the mention of Babylonians once more, for this event occurred one or two generations later and yet these people were still known for being Babylonians (or Parthians), as were Thea Muse and Phraataces.

Philip, the grandson of Zamaris, still appears to have had his cavalry forces, but the mountain-top citadel of Gamala, which was just mentioned, is most definitely not a place for 500 mounted archers. Cavalry were the light tanks of the Roman and Medieval army and their whole rationale was built around their mobility and manoeuvrability; to surprise the enemy with their speed; to dash in, strike and retire, ready to strike again at will. To locate such a mobile force among the goat-tracks of a precipitous mountain – and this citadel of Gamala is truly precipitous – would be madness in the extreme. I have no doubt that Zamaris would have chosen the city of Gamala on the plains of Aurania (or Bethanya) for his new capital city, rather than the inhospitable slopes of the Gamala citadel.

On the plains of Aurania (Bethanya) there was good grazing for

* Herod Agrippa, a son of Aristobulus, reigned in Bethanya (Aurania) after the death of Herod Philip in AD 37. He also took over the rule of Galilee-Israel after the death of Herod Antipas in AD 39.

goats and sheep, while the fertile, volcanic soil that covers the undulating hills around Umm el-Jimal is also good for growing grain – despite the low rainfall. Even today, the rolling hills around the city are cultivated with grain; and while the resulting crop-yields would not be as dense as among the south downs of England, there are large areas of land to be farmed in the modern Hauran. In addition, the irrigation systems the newcomers had built around the town of Umm el-Jimal probably afforded the farming of a few cash crops, just as some of the small farming settlements in the area do today. Indeed, the climate, agriculture, economy and architecture of this Gamala of the plains (Umm el-Jimal) was not unlike the city of Marib in Saba. The history of Marib, and its links with Judaism, have already been debated at length in the book *Solomon*.

In addition, the fortress of Gamala on the plains of Aurania would have allowed Zamaris' (and Philip's) mounted archers to sally out across the fast open ground to strike at an approaching enemy, before retiring once more behind the city's secure walls. These rolling hills are ideal cavalry country, and Judaea's eastern borders would have been much better protected by a frontier town like this Gamala of the plains, than a few frightened forces holed up in a remote mountain-top citadel. It may well be that there were two towns to the east of the Jordan called Gamala, but the mountain-top citadel close to the Sea of Galilee was technically in Gaulanitis. The Gamala of Bethanya (Bethany) and Aurania (Ourania) is much more likely to have been the Gamala of the plains – Umm el-Jimal (Umm el-Gamal).

Fig 26. The ruined city of Umm el-Jimal.

IV *Fourth Sect of Judaism*

The fourth creed

This link between the historical Bethanya and the biblical Bethany means that the whole thrust of the biblical texts shift eastwards. The traditional interpretation of the New Testament is that nearly all of the events took place in either Jerusalem or Galilee. But now it would seem that some of these references to Galilee may pertain to a revolutionary sect, or perhaps even to a circling ritual; and it would also appear that many of the key players in the biblical saga were actually associated with the province of Bethanya, which lies to the east of the river Jordan. This growing and compelling link between the Parthians in Bethanya, Judas of Gamala, Jesus of Gamala and many of the prime characters in the New Testament narrative is very interesting; so perhaps we should look further at the aims and ambitions of this Judas of Gamala.

Perhaps the most important aspect in the accounts, regarding Judas of Gamala, is that he set up an entirely new sect of Judaism. What we were looking for, in our quest to find the true ancestry of Jesus, was a radical secular and religious leader who started a new Judaic philosophy in the early part of the first century AD, and here in the accounts of Judas of Gamala we find exactly such an individual:

> For Judas ... who created a <u>fourth</u> philosophic sect among us, and had a great many followers therein, filled our civil government with tumults ... by this system of philosophy, which we were before unacquainted. [J12]

In his comprehensive account of first century Judaea, the historian Josephus Flavius diligently notes the beliefs of the three main sects of Judaism – the Pharisees, the Sadducees and the Essene. It was always a problem trying to decide to which of these sects the biblical Jesus belonged. However, here we have a new 'fourth sect' that appears to be equally as radical as the Essene and very similar indeed to the creed of Jesus and James. Josephus' discourse on this fourth sect of Judaism indicates that they were similar to the Pharisees, but that they valued liberty and dedication to god and would call no man 'lord'. They were also said to be unafraid of death and demonstrated an indifference to pain. Does any of this sound familiar?

The sect that Jesus and his brother James led has always appeared to have had similarities with and links to the radical Essene sect who resided at the desert 'monastery' of Qumran; especially as a number of Zealots were numbered among the biblical disciples, including Simon Zelotes (Simon the Zealot, who was probably Simon the Leper). However, as we have seen, the principal compatriot of Judas of Gamala was one Sadduc, a name which, in its original Hebrew spelling, is the name Zadok. As it happens, the Manual of Discipline in the Dead Sea Scrolls calls the Essene sect the Sons of Zadok, and so the Essene may have been a later, even more radical, offshoot of Judas' 'fourth creed'. If the Church of Jesus was related to, or the same as, the fourth Judaic sect of Judas of Gamala, then it should be of no surprise that it also displayed similarities with one of its later offshoots. This similarity would also strengthen the links between Judas of Gamala and Jesus of Gamala [the biblical Jesus].

The fourth sect of Judaism sprang from the tax-free province of Bethanya (Aurania) to the east of the river Jordan, which had originally been settled by Zamaris [Phraataces and Thea Muse Ourania]. Given the tax-free status of this province, it is not surprising that the primary complaint of the later Judas of Gamala, the founding father of the fourth sect, was in regard to the new Roman taxes that were being imposed upon the region by the Roman consul Cyrenius. In a similar fashion, when the Jerusalem priesthood tried to entrap Jesus, the primary question was again on the subject of taxes:

> Then went the Pharisees, and took counsel how they might entangle him in his talk. Tell us therefore, What thinkest thou? Is it lawful to give tribute (taxes) unto Caesar, or not? But Jesus perceived their wickedness, and said ... Render therefore unto Caesar the things which are Caesar's; and unto God the things that are God's. [B13]

Note that Jesus did not necessarily believe what he said, he just 'perceived their wickedness' and gave a typical dissembling, political reply. Perhaps a better illustration of Jesus' thoughts on the matter of taxation is to be found in this quote:

> And when (Jesus) had made a scourge of small cords, he drove them all out of the temple, and the sheep, and the oxen; and poured out the changers' money, and overthrew the tables. [B14]

This may have been an act designed to cleanse the Temple of money-changers, but it was also an act against the tyranny of the collection of tax and interest by the Temple authorities in Jerusalem. This philosophy is again directly in line with the philosophy of the fourth sect of Judas of Gamala, who were protesting about taxation.

Having said this, I have no doubt that Judas of Gamala required taxes of his own to maintain the small kingdom of Bethanya (Aurania) and its independent army, but since he had been promised that Bethanya would remain free from Judaean (and Roman) taxes, he was not about to let that tax-free status be revoked just because there was a new king or governor in Syria.

The teachings of this new fourth sect of Judaism seem to be familiar too. As we have already seen, Josephus Flavius says of them that:

> They say that god is to be their only ruler and lord. [J15]

In other words, it would seem that there was a republican element within the fourth sect of Judaism, and that the high priesthood of Jerusalem, and perhaps even the kingship, were being rejected. But this sentiment is exactly the same as the teachings of Jesus, who reputedly said:

> Then saith Jesus unto him ... thou shalt worship the Lord thy God, and him only shalt thou serve. [B16]

There are further similarities between the biblical Jesus and this 'fourth sect' of Judaism to be found in the account of Jesus, son of Ananus (the son of a priest), who I have already identified with the biblical Jesus in the book *Jesus*. It is said of Jesus ben Ananus that:

> Certain of the most eminent among the populace had great indignation at the dire cry of his ... and gave the man a great number of severe stripes (lashes). Yet he did not either say anything for himself or anything peculiar to those who chastised him, but still went on with the same words he cried before. [J17]

This account has a great deal in common with the scourging of Jesus after his trial, but the indifference to suffering this Jesus displayed again fits rather well with the philosophy of the fourth Judaic sect.

These are not the only similarities, for this revolt against taxation by Judas of Gamala was not a trivial event; it was most certainly not a pavement protest that returned to the inn for a few beers when it got dark. No, Josephus Flavius specifically blames this Judas of Gamala for the entire Jewish Civil War and the eventual destruction of Jerusalem in AD 70.

> All sorts of misfortunes also sprang from these men, and the nation was infected with this doctrine to an incredible degree. One violent war came upon us after another ... there were also great robberies and murders of our principal men ... a famine came upon us which reduced us to the last degree of despair, as did also the taking and demolishing of our cities. Nay, the sedition at last increased so high, that the very Temple of God was burned down... [J18]

Likewise, I have already identified the biblical Jesus as one of the authors of the Jewish Civil War, for the New Testament specifically says that Jesus was a rebel with a large army.

> Think not that I (Jesus) am come to send peace on earth: I came not to send peace, but a sword. [B19]

> Then said (Jesus) unto them, But now, he that hath a purse, let him take it, and likewise his wallet: and he that hath no sword, let him sell his garment, and buy one. [B22]

The arming of the disciples of Jesus was not simply for decoration, so that they could pretend to be Knights of God; instead, this was a real armed uprising arranged and commanded by Jesus himself. The plan was to mount a surprise attack on the Jerusalem priesthood and government and so to take over all of Judaea. Presumably this action would then spark a revolt against Rome and so free Judaeo-Israel from Roman dominion.

> And (Jesus) came out, and went, as he was wont, to the Mount of Olives; and his disciples also followed him ... a band of men and officers from the chief priests and Pharisees, cometh thither with lanterns and torches and weapons ... When they which were about him saw what would follow, they said unto him, Lord, shall we smite with the sword? ... And one of them smote the servant of the high priest, and cut off his right ear ... Then Jesus said unto the chief priests, and captains of the temple, and the elders, which were come to him, do ye come out, as against a Zealot, with swords and staves? [B23]

Note that Jesus was being identified here as a Zealot leader, which he tries to deny; but since the disciple Simon was a Zealot, the authorities were probably correct. [24] This biblical account also makes it appear that this meeting on the Mount of Olives was a trivial gathering of the disciples, who happened to be armed with swords for some strange reason, but the complete account of this event paints a rather different picture:

> ... (the Egyptian prophet) got together thirty thousand men that were deluded by him; these he led round about from the wilderness to the mount which was called the Mount of Olives, and was ready to break into Jerusalem by force from that place; and if he could but once conquer the Roman garrison and the people, he intended to domineer them ... But (the governor) met him with his Roman soldiers, while all the people assisted him in his attack ... when it came to battle the Egyptian ran away, with a few others, while ... the rest of the multitude were dispersed every one to their own homes... [J25]

Here is a real historical account of the 'tumult' that the fourth sect of Judaism had created in Jerusalem. The meeting of the biblical Jesus [the Egyptian False Prophet] on the Mount of Olives was not for prayer or meditation (with swords), but for an armed assault on the city of Jerusalem using an army of some thirty thousand men. The Bible echoes the great magnitude of this event when the Gospel of John says that a *speira* σπειρα of men (a band of men) came to arrest Jesus. But a *speira* is more commonly termed as a *cohort*, and both of these are Roman terms for a tenth of a legion – or some 500 - 600 heavily armed soldiers. Clearly, this was a major insurrection being thwarted by the might of the Roman army, and not a small gathering of disciples being rounded up by a few local 'police constables'.

Note also that Jesus was being called 'the Egyptian', and the evidence for this being so can be seen in the following verse from Acts:

> Art not thou that Egyptian, which before these days made an uproar, and led out into the wilderness four thousand men that were murderers? [B26]

This was Saul (St Paul) being mistaken for the Egyptian False Prophet, but the real Egyptian prince in exile in this era was actually Jesus himself. Quite obviously, this verse from Acts is a simple retelling of the well-known 'loaves and fishes' story, and the proof that this is so is to be found in the term being used for a 'murderer', which was *sicarios* σικαριος. This term refers to the Sicarii, and in this era it was Jesus who was the leader of a band of Sicarii assassins, as we shall see in the next chapter. The equivalent, but toned down and more acceptable, 'loaves and fishes' story says:

> And he said unto them, Come ye yourselves apart into a desert place, and rest a while ... And the people saw them departing, and many knew him, and ran afoot thither out of all cities, and they went out, and came together unto him ... And they sat down in ranks, by hundreds, and by fifties ... And they that did eat of the loaves were about five thousand men. [B27]

Thus we have two very similar tales from the Bible and from Josephus; one regarding the Mount of Olives insurrection, and the other about the leading of the 5,000 into the wilderness. The Synoptic Gospels clearly state that Jesus led both of these events, while Josephus and Acts say that the instigator of both events was the enigmatic 'Egyptian False Prophet'.

Note the similarly evasive nature of the accounts in both Acts and Josephus' *Jewish War*, which is one reason why I have stated that Saul-Josephus was the author of both of these texts. Saul-Josephus was normally very diligent in recording the name of every character in his accounts, and so I am certain that he did know the true name of this 'Egyptian'; thus his reluctance to give the Egyptian's true name in his secular books and also in Acts suggests the possibility of a deliberate cover-up. Robert Eisenman, the renowned theologian, says of these two accounts and the suspicious cover-up:

> We will note many such suspicious overlaps in the data available to us. [28]

Eisenman then goes on to make a similar comparison between Jesus and Judas of Gamala:

> Luke's version (of the little apocalypse) is introduced by reference to the destruction of the Temple and generally refers to famine, wars and sectarian strife ... These (are similar to) a section in *Antiquities*, in which Josephus describes the woes brought upon the people by the movement founded by Judas the Galilean (Judas of Gamala). [29]

Again, we can see a direct comparison between the Church of Jesus and the fourth sect of Judas of Gamala. This was not Judas himself creating these woes, as we have moved on a generation here, but it would seem that the sect that Judas had founded was being continued and furthered by the biblical Jesus himself. This would not be so surprising if Jesus was the son of Judas of Gamala.

The obvious reason for Saul-Josephus' infuriating silence regarding the true identity of the 'Egyptian False Prophet' was that this character was actually Jesus himself. But for many reasons it was deemed unacceptable to let the followers of Saul-Josephus, the proto-Christians, know the true heritage of their 'saviour'. But Jesus was Egyptian, which is why the Gospel of Matthew says of Jesus: 'Out of Egypt I have called my Son'. [B30] Once more, the evidence demonstrates that Jesus was of Egyptian descent, and we can now see compelling evidence to demonstrate that this royal heritage was gained via the illustrious line of Thea Muse Ourania.

Philip

The evidence explored so far would seem to suggest that the biblical Jesus was associated with, or perhaps even the leader of, this fourth sect of Judaism that had been founded in about AD 7 by Zamaris (the Parthian or Babylonian Jew), who may well have been one and the same as Judas of Gamala. This sect was then continued by Jesus of Gamala, who I have previously identified as the biblical Jesus. In other words, the fourth sect was the group who are known in the New Testament as the Zelots ζηλωτης. The term *zealos* ζηλος is supposed to refer to those who were zealous for the law (of Moses), but it can also refer to jealousy. An alternative term that was used for the Zelots, according to the biblical Concordance, was Canaanite, a term that can again refer to jealousy. However, the latter word, *canaanite,* was also derived from the Hebrew *quanna* קנא meaning 'possessor' or 'purchaser', with the inference being that this term actually refers to a banker. Since the whole dispute between Judas of Gamala and the authorities revolved around who had the right to levy taxes, the fourth sect may have also been known as 'bankers' for taxes as well as 'zealots' for the law.

We know that Jesus' sect included Zealots in their number, as one of the disciples was called Simon Zelotes, and it was Simon who was also called the Canaanite (because the two terms are interchangeable). We also know that Simon (probably Simon the Leper) was the name of one of Jesus' brothers:

> Is not this the carpenter's son? Is not his mother called Mary? And his brethren, James, and Joses, and Simon, and Judas? [B32]

Even the most eminent of theologians, like Robert Eisenman and Adam Clarke, understand and admit that these were the true siblings of Jesus, and not simply fellow brothers in a cause or society. So the brothers of Jesus were named James, Joses, Simon and Judas, and yet these names were also among Jesus' twelve disciples. But this nominative similarity gives us an interesting possibility and, as I have shown in my previous works, the inescapable conclusion is that many of the disciples were actually the blood-brothers of Jesus. However, these same names give us yet another possibility – a direct link between the biblical Jesus and Judas of Gamala. Josephus Flavius says of the latter:

> Besides this, the sons of Judas the Galilean (Judas of Gamala) were executed; I mean that they were the sons of that Judas who caused the people to revolt when Quirinius (Cyrenius) came to take an account of the estates of the Jews. The names of those sons were James and Simon, whom Alexander commanded to be crucified. [33]

James and Simon were, of course, both names of the brothers of Jesus. But this similarity would imply that Judas of Gamala and Joseph the father of Jesus were the same person. So is this possible? Well, the date of the revolution started by Judas of Gamala was the same as the birth date of Jesus. The next generation of revolutionaries to come from Gamala, as we have already seen, were led by someone called Jesus. Thus both Judas of Gamala and the later Jesus of Gamala came from the province of Bethanya (Bethany), which was a favourite location for the biblical Jesus, and both of these revolutionaries appeared to control a substantial private army.

This may initially have seemed like an impossible condition for the biblical Jesus to have met; however, the biblical account of Jesus' armed assault from the Mount of Olives proves beyond doubt that the biblical Jesus *was* the leader of a substantial army, just as Jesus of Gamala was. Josephus says of Jesus of Gamala (and Jesus of Sapphias):

> Jesus the son of Sapphias, who we have already mentioned as the leader of a seditious tumult of mariners and poor people.

> Simon the son of Gamiel, persuaded the high priests and Jesus the son of Gamala and others of this seditious faction, to cut me down (reduce Josephus Flavius' power).

> A certain Galilean then stayed at Jerusalem whose name was Jesus, who had about him a band of six hundred armed men. [J34]

Thus, Jesus of Gamala (and Jesus of Sapphias) still controlled a large army long after the initial exile of Zamaris to Judaeo-Syria. But since this army was comprised of fishermen (mariners), and the sign of Christianity was the fish, this just has to be a reference to the armed faction controlled and led by the biblical Jesus. Thus Jesus of Gamala (and Jesus of Sapphias) were one and the same as the biblical Jesus.

Likewise, if Zamaris really was one and the same as Judas of Gamala, then we might expect that his sons also controlled a large army. That is exactly what we find, for it is said of Judas of Gamala's grandson, Philip:

> ... there was a firm friendship between him and King Agrippa (Agrippa II of Chalcis, Syria). He also had an army which he maintained, as great as that of a king; which he exercised and led wheresoever he had occasion to march. [J35]

Here was Philip of Gamala in charge a vast army that had free rein over the lands of Syria (Bethanya and Aurania) and also over the lands of Galilee. But a vast army 'as great as that of a king' needs a great deal of funds to maintain it, and these funds were only available because Zamaris [Judas of Gamala] founded a colony in Judaeo-Syria [at Umm el-Jimal] that was free of taxation from both Rome and Jerusalem. This means that Judas of Gamala had to be a tax collector – a collector of his own taxes to fund his private army. It was for this reason that complaints were being made about Jesus being surrounded by tax collectors:

> And it came to pass, as Jesus sat amongst them in the house, behold, many publicans and sinners came and sat down with him and his disciples. [B36]

As is usual, one has to decipher the text to make sense of it. The term being used for a 'publican' is actually a *telones* τελωνης, which means 'tax collector' – and this is a term that seems to have very little to do with the brewery trade, so the translation of 'publican' is highly misleading. In fact, just to emphasise this point, the term *harmartolos* αμαρτωλος for 'sinner' can also mean a 'tax collector'. However, having already noted the possibility of the Zelots being linked with banking, it is likely that these tax collectors were also bankers.

These tax collectors, whom Jesus associated with, probably included his parents. The biblical Concordance says that the name Cleophas κλωπας is exactly the same as the name Alphaeus αλφαιος, which again demonstrates that many of the disciples were actually Jesus' brothers, as I argued in the book *Jesus*. [Alphaeus was the father of James, the brother of Jesus.] However, it also says that both of these names mean 'exchange', from the Hebrew *chelep* חלף meaning 'exchange'. What the Concordance does not do is explain what, exactly, was being exchanged. Bearing in mind the clear inference from the evidence already explored, the exchange referred to has to be of money, and so Alphaeus-Cleophas was an exchequer – a tax collector.

So Jesus was accused by his contemporaries of associating with (and being related to) tax collectors, or moneylenders. It has often been assumed that the people's horror at this association between Jesus and tax collectors was due to tax collectors being a thoroughly nasty collection of people. The theologian Adam Clarke makes this very point when he says:

> It is certain that those who fear god should not associate, through choice, with the workers of iniquity, and should only be found with them when transacting their secular business requires it, or when they have the prospect of doing good to their souls. [37]

However, this new analysis of Jesus' status gives us another possibility entirely. The 'people' who objected were most probably the Jerusalem elders and administrators, and so their 'horror' may have been based upon the fact that Judas of Gamala had not paid any taxes (or Temple dues?) for several decades. Thus Judas and his offspring were in a position to fund their own army and remain wholly independent of the Judaean authorities. The Jerusalem hierarchy had a tax-haven on their doorstep, and they were none too pleased about this situation (except, perhaps, if the Parthian army advanced from the east – then they would have asked Judas of Gamala what he proposed to do about it). But the elders could do nothing about the situation, as this eastern province and its standing army and cavalry were far too strong for them to deal with.

Here was Judas of Gamala's son, Jesus of Gamala [the biblical Jesus], and he too was following in the same tradition of maintaining his own tax collectors, who channelled the taxes of Bethanya and Aurania towards Gamala and not towards Jerusalem. This was probably the reason for Jesus overturning the tables of the moneylenders in the Temple of Jerusalem. Perhaps the Temple was overstepping its remit, by raising secular taxes as well as its own Temple dues. Jesus, as tax collector for Bethanya in Syria, would have had a vested interest in opposing any authority that was encroaching on his own tax collections.

This line of research and argument does seem to make a great deal of sense. But if is true then we need to amalgamate several of the characters in the various texts that deal with this era. These amalgamations are:

Josephus *Antiquities*		**Josephus *Life***		**Bible**
Zamaris, Babylonian Jew	=	Judas of Gamala	=	Joseph, father of Jesus
??	=	Jesus of Gamala	=	Jesus, son of Joseph
Simon of Gamiel	=	Simon, son of Judas	=	Simon, son of Joseph
Jacim, son of Zamaris	=	James, son of Judas	=	James, son of Joseph
Philip, son of Jacim	=	??	=	Philip the disciple

Note that the name 'James' in the New Testament is simply a rather poor translation of the Greek Jacobos Ιακωβος or the Hebrew Jacob יעקב. Thus the name Jacim appears to be a cross between the names Jacob and James.

While it may seem unlikely that Josephus Flavius had mis-identified so many names in his records, this may have been a deliberate deception. Remember that I have previously argued that Jesus of Gamala, Jesus of Sapphias, Jesus Ananus and the biblical Jesus were all revolutionaries from Judaeo-Syria, who led large armed followings during the middle of the first century AD. Can we really believe that so many revolutionaries called Jesus were all competing to overthrow the Judaic authorities in Jerusalem? Or is it more rational to believe that Josephus has used different titles for the same person, presumably to confuse the history of the region and thus to separate the revolutionary aspect of the biblical Jesus from his more orthodox pacific persona. Note also that the different names in the table above occur substantially in different books of Josephus, so the presence of a different team of scribes may well be another factor in this.

However, if these various nominative associations are true, then it would make Jesus a much more important character in the wider politics of this region during this era. But that is what I have been saying all along. Jesus always did appear to have royal pretensions, many influential and well-connected friends and an extensive power base – and now we know why. Had Jesus been the son of Judas of Gamala [Zamaris], then he would have been the son of the leader of Judaea's fourth religious sect. This would have been a powerful position in its own right, but had Judas of Gamala [Zamaris] also been related to, or a pseudonym for, King Phraataces, then Jesus would indeed have had royal pretensions too. Such an ancestry would explain a great deal about the events of the New Testament.

But if the biblical Jesus and his extended family were directly related to and descended from Queen Thea Muse and King Phraataces, then an explanation must be sought for the Judaic-sounding names they chose to use in the New Testament accounts. Thea Muse and Phraataces were of the Egyptian and Parthian royal line respectively, so why would their descendants have used 'Judaic' names? The answer to this problem is that the biblical names we are familiar with may seem to be Judaic to us, as we are conditioned to believe this by the religious authorities. However, in actual fact, these names are not Judaic at all and the vast majority of them can be traced back into ancient Egypt, as we shall see. But this is an extensive topic that will have to be explored in a later chapter.

Stable

We have seen historical evidence that an Egypto-Parthian royal family were exiled to Bethanya (Jordano-Syria) in about AD 4, and also that a new Judaic sect appeared in this same location in about AD 7. It has also been demonstrated that many of these events and characters can be directly linked to the biblical Jesus, whose family was also said to have been forced to travel to a new location in AD 7 because of the taxation by Cyrenius (Quirinius). This forced exile and subsequent long and arduous journey of the Parthian royal family would help explain the reasoning behind the mythology that Jesus was born in a stable. Matthew says that Jesus was born in a guesthouse, but Luke is the author who places the Christmas-card gloss on the tale by saying:

> And she brought forth her firstborn son, and wrapped him in swaddling clothes, and laid him in a manger; because there was no room for them in the inn. [B38]

Whether it was a house or an inn, the general thrust of these stories is that this 'royal' birth was no great state occasion, and so it is entirely possible that the biblical family was on the move. But what was the reason for this great journey? Did entire families really have to travel vast distances across Judaea simply because there was a census and taxation being implemented by a Roman governor?

Initially, the classical biblical story of a 'royal' birth in humble surroundings sounds unlikely in the extreme. But since we now know that Thea Muse and Phraataces were forced into exile at about this same time, the reason for a royal birth in a 'guesthouse' or 'stable' becomes more understandable. Queen Thea Muse Ourania was no longer in her sumptuous royal palace in Parthia, and so the surroundings for this royal birth would indeed have been something to take note of.

Alternatively, the term for 'inn', *kataluma* καταλυμα, also means 'dining room'. As we have already seen, the houses at Umm el-Jimal [Gamala] were made with animal stables downstairs and the dining room upstairs. Since these houses were small rustic abodes, rather than the vast palaces that Thea Muse and Phraataces had previously been used to, it is likely that the upstairs rooms were greatly encumbered with former royal belongings. In the circumstances, it may have been easier to throw the animals out onto the street for a day or two than to arrange for a birth in a cluttered upstairs room.

Either way, the newly exiled and impoverished status of Queen Thea Muse and King Phraataces is one of the few ways we can make sense of the New Testament accounts. I had long suspected that Jesus was of royal blood, but I could not explain exactly why this royal prince would have been born in such lowly surroundings, let alone find a suitable candidate for such a lowly royal birth. However, we now seem to have all the requirements to explain the stable-and-manger birth of a royal prince, with the added bonus that this same birth may well have occurred in AD 7 in Bethanya – or, in other words, at exactly the right moment in history and in exactly the right location.

Magi

Yet again, it seems more and more likely that Jesus was born of the family of Thea Muse and Phraataces, and it is this direct link between Jesus and Parthia that forms the foundations of a very famous biblical event – which goes some way towards finally proving that the true origins of Jesus and his family lie with Thea Muse Ourania:

> Now when Jesus was born in Bethlehem of Judaea in the days of Herod the

> king, behold, there came wise men from the east to Jerusalem. Saying, Where is he that is born King of the Jews? For we have seen his star in the east, and are come to worship him. [B39]

It is entirely possible that this story of the star that the 'wise men' followed to Israel is a simple retelling of the legends of King Solomon, of whom it is said:

> And after he slept, there appeared a brilliant sun, and it came down and shed exceedingly great splendour over Israel. [KN42]

These stars or suns seem to be closely linked to the bloodline of Israel, and signify the appearance of a prince of the realm. These allusions are probably derived from the titles of the Judaic kings and queens, as the title 'Sheba' means 'star'. In the book *Solomon* I demonstrate that not only was King Solomon's queen known as 'Sheba' (the Queen of Sheba), but so was King Solomon's father, King David. The title of 'star', especially among the Hyksos-Judaic queens, alluded to the Queen of Heaven, a title that has already been explored in some detail.

Fig 27. A Zoroastrian faravahar, or depiction of the soul. This motif is obviously taken from the image of the Egyptian flying Sun-disk of Ra.

However, this biblical story about wise men coming from the east has always been a bit of a mystery to me, for these 'wise men' were actually the Persian (or Parthian) *Magus* μαγος: the Magi. The Gospel of Luke has shepherds visiting the birth of Jesus, instead of the Magi; but this term may simply refer to the Hyksos Shepherd Kings. Alternatively, it is also possible that the term being used here for 'shepherd', the Greek *poimen* ποιμην, can be translated as the 'king's counsellors'. Not every shepherd looks after sheep, as the Catholic pope will attest to – and even god is called a shepherd on occasions.

These Magi, or 'wise men' in the King James translation, became the 'three kings' of popular biblical mythology. But this title of 'king' is simply a modern gloss that has no historical foundation whatsoever, and the original designation for the 'wise men' was the three Magi. The biblical Concordance

Plate 1. The Death of Cleopatra. Jean-Andre Rixens, Musee des Augustins, Toulouse, France.

Plate 2. Adoration of the Magi. Pieter Aertsen, Rijksmuseum, Amsterdam. Mary wears her traditional blue tunic, representing the Muse Ourania's association with the sky and the Cosmos.

Plate 3. The Virgin Mary depicted as Muse Ourania, Gornji Grad Cathedral, Slovenia. Note the twelve stars around her head and the Moon at her feet.

Plate 4. Virgin Mary depicted as Muse Ourania. The pose is taken from description in Revelations 12:1, with the twelve stars on a blue background being adopted as the emblem of the EU.

Plate 5. Muse Ourania [Mary] and Calliope. Simon Vouet, Samuel Kress Collection, National Gallery of Art, Washington D.C.

Plate 6. The Beth Alpha zodiac, Israel; taken from a third century AD synagogue.

Plate 7. The Sultan Tekesh mausoleum in Kunya Urgench.

Plate 8. The mausoleum of Jubba II and Cleopatra Selene, daughter of Cleopatra VII, in Kolea, Algeria. The design incorporates mathematical allusions to the Sun and Moon.

Plate 9. The ruined city of Umm el-Jimal in Aurania (Hauran) – the 'Mother of Egypt' and the probable birth-place of the biblical Jesus.

Plates 10-17.
Top row 10-12:
Augustus Caesar, Julius Caesar, Vespasian. British Museum, London.

Second row 13-15:
Cleopatra VII, coin of Cleopatra VII, Thea Muse Ourania. British Museum London, and National Museum of Iran.

Coins 16 & 17:
Two coins (obverse and reverse) of King Phraataces and Queen Thea Muse Ourania. Note that King Phraataces wears a triple torq, probably of gold, and has a prominent wart of the forehead. The royal 'wart' on the forehead is a distinctive identifier of the Phraates kings, but no equivalent of this feature appears in the biblical record.

indicates that the Persian original of this Greek word was *meguceen*, or a 'Worshipper of Fire', from which we derive the English word magician. The Magi were said to be the hereditary priesthood of the Medes, who can be identified with the modern Kurds. The Magi have also been linked to the Mandaeans, the Marsh Arabs from southeastern Iraq who were so mercilessly persecuted by Saddam Hussein. E S Drower says of the Mandaeans:

> Arab authors have sometimes confounded the Mandaeans with the Magi or Magicians, and not without reason, since the cults are very similar. [43]

Finally, the Magi are also closely linked with the Zoroastrian priests who were the followers of the Prophet Zoroaster (Zoroastra); or, for admirers of Richard Strauss, the more familiar pronunciation is Zarathustra – hence the symphony *Also Sprach Zarathustra,* which was used so effectively in the film *2001, A Space Odyssey*. It is probably from the Zoroastrian temples of fire in Baku, Azerbaijan – which contain eternal flames fed by natural gas seeping from the ground – that the title 'Worshipper of Fire' was derived. However, the name Zoroaster is more likely to have been derived from the Hebrew *asther* אסתר and the Greek *aster* αστηρ meaning 'star'.

The influential Magi were said to hold profound and extraordinary religious knowledge and, in a similar fashion to the biblical Joseph and Daniel, the Magi therefore became supreme advisors to the Persian kings. In fact, since Daniel became an advisor to a Persian king, he too would have been a Magi. Indeed, the name given to Daniel was Rab Mag רב-מג which is a Hebrew-Persian compound title that refers to a 'Great Magi'. In this civil capacity the Magi therefore became the counsellors of the royal court, the civil administrators and viziers to the king or queen, as was the biblical Joseph. The Magi eventually formed the upper house of the 'Persian Council of the Megistanes', and it is from this latter title and function that the English term 'magistrate' is derived. Thus the Magi became royal courtiers, or 'court officials' in much the same way as we would understand that term – magistrates and judges.

There was one other important function of the Magi or *megistanes*, and that was the selection and anointing of the next king of Parthia. So what, then, were three Parthian (Persian) king-makers doing in Syrio-Judaea, searching for the next King of the Jews? When using the classical New Testament interpretation of Jesus being a lowly Jewish artisan, the presence of Parthian king-makers at his birth makes absolutely no sense whatsoever. Even the novel addition of Jesus' possible Egyptian ancestry adds little light to the situation, for the Egyptians and Parthians were not exactly the best of friends in this era and the Parthian (Persian) Magi would have had no interest whatsoever in the birth of an Egyptian prince. However, if Jesus was descended from Thea Muse and Phraataces then everything suddenly becomes crystal clear.

King Phraataces and Queen Thea Muse Ourania had been the king and queen of Parthia from AD 2 until they were dethroned in AD 4. This may have been a short and turbulent reign, but they were nevertheless king and queen of Parthia (and Thea Muse had been queen of Parthia for about 25 years prior to this), as the numismatic (coin) evidence proves.

Following their exile from Parthia, Rome took the opportunity of installing one of Phraates IV's exiled sons back onto the throne of Parthia. Augustus' first attempt was the installation of Orodes III, but Josephus says that he was deposed within two years due to his extreme cruelty. If Thea Muse and Phraataces were deposed in AD 4 and a year had passed before Orodes III took over the monarchy from them, then the Parthian throne would have been vacant once more around AD 7, when Orodes III was deposed. However, AD 7 is the very date of the Roman taxation of Judaea and thus the very date that the Gospel of Luke claims for the birth of the biblical Jesus. With the dethronement of Orodes III in AD 7, the Parthian Magi would have been on the lookout for a new king from the royal bloodline of the Parthian Arsacid dynasty. While Thea Muse and Phraataces may have been dethroned, due to their unorthodox Egyptian-style marriage, a son (or grandson) of theirs would still have been an Arsacid Parthian prince – and it was for this reason that the Parthian Magi travelled all the way to Judaeo-Syria to see for themselves this new Parthian prince.

So far, so good. We now have a clear and irrefutable link between Jesus and the Parthian royalty, but then something peculiar happens in the biblical accounts. It is said that Herod (the Great) heard of the Magi's visit to Bethanya and desired to speak to them. The Magi said that they had come to worship the 'King of the Jews', which was a deliberate slight on Herod's own kingship, as he was the King of the Jews at the time. As mentioned previously, for these dates to tie up correctly this king must have been Herod Archelous or Herod Philip (the next generation) rather than Herod the Great. Also, the term being used for 'worship' in this verse has been badly translated by some zealous Christian scribes, who were desperately trying to turn Jesus into a godlet. The original word was *proskuneo* προσκυνεω, meaning 'kiss the hand', and this more accurately describes the true intent and actions of the Parthian Magi king-makers. Being loyal courtiers, they would indeed have made their greetings by kissing the hand of the newborn Parthian prince.

But it is said that this Herod was outraged by the news of a newborn 'King of the Jews' and so he ordered the slaughter of all the infants in Bethlehem:

> Then Herod, when he saw that he was mocked of the Magi, was exceeding wroth, and sent forth, and slew all the children that were in Bethlehem, and in all the coasts thereof, from two years old and under, according to the time which he had diligently enquired of the Magi. B44

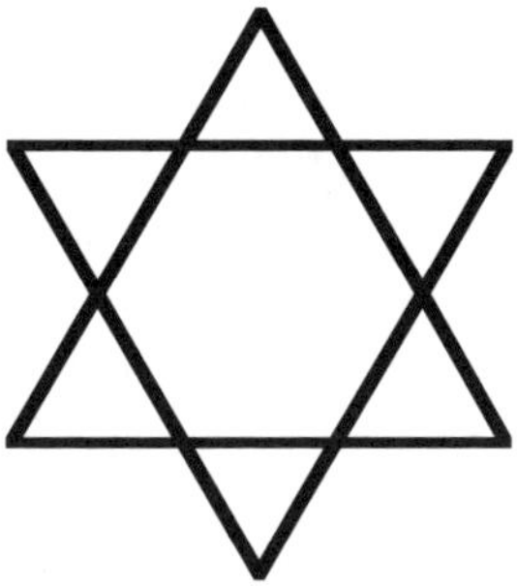

Fig 28. The six-sided Magen David.

In the book *Jesus* I have already identified this slaughter with Herod the Great's slaughter of his own children in a bloody royal accession dispute. However, if the Herod in question was actually Herod Archelous or Herod Philip, then perhaps there was another fit of royal rage and retribution, and the accounts of this incident were modelled on the indiscriminate infanticide of Herod the Great.

In this case, the mention of the town of Bethlehem in this verse may be a little misleading, as it may not be the town in Judaea just to the south of Jerusalem. The original name of Bethlehem was based upon the Greek Bethleem βηθλεεμ, which was in turn based upon the Hebrew name Beth-Lechem בית-לחם, which is said to mean 'House of Bread'. However, if we are now assuming that some of the biblical lexicon is being influenced by Egypto-Parthian terms, then we may be looking for a Persian/Arabic equivalent instead. In this case the name of Beth-Lechem may well have been derived from Baith al Chemya, meaning the 'House of Alchemy'.

Alchemy can be explained as the early science of chemistry and physics, and if any of the priests of the primary religions of this era were dabbling in alchemical esoterica, it was the Magi. However, this is not the true origin of this word for it actually goes back into Egypt, where Kam  was the original name for Egypt itself. Thus Al Chemy is simply an Arabic term meaning 'The Egypt' and referring more specifically to 'The Egyptian Arts'; because the basics of modern chemistry and physics came out of Egypt. Indeed, it is often claimed that the term 'chemistry' was derived directly from Kam , the ancient name for Egypt. If this were the case, then Bethlehem may actually refer to 'The House of the Egyptians', with the term 'house' possibly referring to the royal family. There was only one Egyptian royal family in Judaea at this time, and that was the family of Thea Muse Ourania.

But if the term 'alchemy' came out of Egypt rather than Persia (Parthia), then so may the term Magi. The biblical Concordance and the

Hebrew dictionary indicate that Magi is not a Hebrew word, and point instead towards Persia. However, I think that this assessment may be in error. In fact, the word Magi is Hebrew, for it forms a part of the 'Star Prophecy' of the New Testament Magi, who followed the 'star' to Jerusalem. The star in question must have been the Magen David מגן דוד or the Star of David, for the Magi were following the *magen*, or star. However, to be more precise, the Hebrew *magen* מגן actually means 'shield', but this word has been translated as 'star' because the Star of David does indeed look like a star.

The answer to this muddle is that the 'star' on the flag of Israel is actually composed of two interlocking triangles or pyramids (one being inverted). In addition, the Hebrew word *mag* is the prefix for the Hebrew word *magdal* מגדל meaning 'tower', which was originally derived from the Egyptian *maktal* *(maktar)* or *magadal* *(magadar)* meaning 'tower' – and from which the New Testament also derives the title Magdalene.

It was from the symbology of the interlocking pyramids, which form the outline of the Star of David, that the star imagery for the goddess Isis was derived. The star / pyramid symbology of Isis is not so well known; however, a chapel of Psusennes II at Giza was dedicated to 'Isis, Mistress of the Pyramids'. [45] Likewise, it is from the name Isis, who was called Ast or Est in Egyptian, that the Phoenician goddess Astarte was derived. Astarte may well have been a Lunar goddess but she was also known as the Queen of Heaven and linked to the morning and evening star, Venus. That there must have been a strong association between Astarte and stars can be seen in the Hebrew word *ester* or *aster* אסתר meaning 'star'.

Fig 30. Helen of Sparta wearing a Phrygian (Trojan) cap.

Funnily enough, a related word *eser* אסר or *atsar* עצר means 'magistrate', the same as the Persian Magi, and so *aster* and Magi both relate to stars and magistrates. Thus the Magi in the New Testament were not simply looking for the planet Venus in the (western) evening sky, they were also looking for an incarnation of Isis (Esther or Astarte) the star goddess. Mary, the mother of Jesus, was that star (or incarnation of Isis) and this is a name that has endured through the ages, even if the etymology does not always fully support it. The true origin of the name Miraim (Mary) is given in a later chapter, but here is a small quote regarding the mythology of Mary the 'Sea Star':

> Here a word has to be added concerning the explanation for *stella maris*, the Star of the Sea. It is more popular than any other interpretation of the name 'Mary', and is dated back to St. Jerome. But the great doctor of the Church knew Hebrew too well to translate the first syllable of the name *miryam* by star; in Isaiah 40:15, he renders the word *stilla* (a drop), not *stella* (a star). [46]

In conclusion, it is likely that the Persian title of 'Magi' was originally an Egyptian term that had been derived from the great 'towers' of Egypt, which still stand on the Giza plateau to this day. I have already attempted to show that the ancient guardians of the pyramids were also the guardians of many of the secrets of Egyptian theology, astronomy, metrology, architecture and science. The Giza temple complex was the cornerstone of Egyptian esoteric knowledge, as it still is today with its peculiar depiction on the Great Seal of America and its strong association with Masonry. If anything was to represent the origins of the Magi's illustrious title, it would have to be the Great Pyramid of Egypt rather than a simple flame.

Liberty

Incidentally, it has long been suspected that the Statue of Liberty was conceived as a representation of Isis-Astarte, the Queen of Heaven. The sculptor of the statue was Frederic Bartholdi, while Gustave Eiffel designed the supporting structure, and the entire sculpture was made in France between 1876 and 1884. However, during the French Revolution a century before, the new Republic had decided that the seal of state would be a female 'goddess' figure complete with spear and Phrygian cap, which was a favourite headdress of Helen of Sparta (Helen of Troy). This mythical French heroine became known as Marianne, the icon of liberty, but the link here to the biblical Mariame (Mary) and to Isis is inescapable.

So who was the model for this French (American) icon of Isis, the lady of liberty? The face on the statue is actually that of a rather stern, masculine-looking woman with bold features. It has long been thought that the model for this was Bartholdi's mother, but could there have been an alternative model? Egypt had been opened up by Napoleon a century before this time and the iconography of Egypt was very popular in this era. In addition, the heavily masonic world of American politics and business would have been very happy to push for an icon of Isis to be a national symbol for all America. Was an image of a goddess or a queen from this era of Egyptian discovery used instead? Some of the busts attributed to Cleopatra show a similar masculine profile, while the cloth headdress that she sometimes wears also looks vaguely familiar. Was Isis-Cleopatra chosen to become the face of Liberty?

Fig 31. Bustof Cleopatra Selene

The face of the Statue of Liberty.

Out of Egypt

Following the visit of the Magi, the very next verses in the Gospel of Matthew relate the flight of Jesus and his family into Egypt:

> And when they were departed, behold, the angel of the lord appears to Joseph in a dream, saying, Arise, and take the young child and his mother, and flee into Egypt, and be thou there until I bring thee word: for Herod will seek the young child to destroy him. When he arose, he took the young child and his mother by night, and departed into Egypt. And was there until the death of Herod: that it might be fulfilled which was spoken of the lord by the prophet, saying, 'Out of Egypt have I called my son'. [B47]

These accounts now give us a new problem, for having decided that Jesus may well have been a Parthian prince, his parents decide to take him to Egypt for safety. Just why would the mother of a Parthian prince, who had been visited by the Magi of Parthia, decide that Egypt was a much safer location for her child than Parthia?

Well, one of the beauties of the thesis that has been explored thus far is that it can easily explain all of these diverse problems. The Persian (Parthian) Magi came to see Jesus because he was a Parthian prince, as we have just seen. However, his mother may well have decided that Parthia was not exactly the safest place for their new child, as the royal family had only just been exiled from that empire. But this royal family did have other options and alternative supporters in other countries – for Thea Muse Ourania was the lost daughter of Cleopatra VII. In the circumstances, perhaps Egypt was the safest place for this royal prince, and this choice would give the double benefit of allowing him to gain a first-class royal education at the great Temple of Heliopolis and to explore the great libraries of Alexandria.

In science, theories are only deemed to be true when they have the power of solving additional problems, both retrospectively and predictively. This thesis is beginning to solve any number of intractable problems that have lain unexplained for millennia. Thus we are on course towards proving that the biblical Jesus was directly related to Queen Thea Muse Ourania.

V

Judaic Names?

The task at the beginning of this book was to attempt to discover members of an exiled royal family who were living in Syrio-Judaea around the turn of the first century AD, who may have had strong links to the great royal dynasties of Egypt and Parthia, and who could be linked to the biblical texts in some manner. That task is now complete, and we appear to have discovered our royal biblical family. However, there is still one rather troubling aspect to this radical new identification – the names traditionally given to the biblical family.

Most readers will be familiar enough with the New Testament to realise that the father of Jesus was not called Phraataces, and his mother was not called Thea Muse Ourania (nor Cleopatra, for that matter). On the face of it, this would seem to be a major stumbling block; for if this entire thesis is true in any way, then it would seem that this Egypto-Parthian royal family would have had to have adopted Judaic names after they were exiled to Judaea. But it is highly unlikely that this would have happened. Thea Muse and Phraataces were not Jews, as such, and it would seem unlikely in the extreme that they would convert to Judaism just because of their exile.

Initially, this might all seem very logical, but only because we have been conditioned into thinking in a very constrained manner. Our perception, which has been fostered and nurtured by all of our educational authorities, is that the Jews were the Jews, and although they lived in a sea of other Middle Eastern nations, they remained completely separate from these other people. This, however, is nonsense. In all of my other books I have tried to demonstrate the close links that once existed between the Jews and the Lower Egyptians – indeed, most of the biblical patriarchs and kings were actually pharaohs of Egypt, who sometimes ruled over a united

Egypto-Judaic nation. Strabo confirms these close links between Egypt and Judaea at the turn of the first century when he says:

> This region lies towards the north; and it is inhabited ... by mixed stocks of people from Egyptian and Arabian and Phoenician tribes ... But though the inhabitants are mixed up thus, the most prevalent of the accredited reports in regard to the Temple at Jerusalem, represents the ancestors of the present Judaeans as Egyptians. [S1]

This was why my first book on this subject was entitled *Jesus, Last of the Pharaohs*, for it seemed obvious that the New Testament family was closely related to the Egyptian royal line. The further revelations in this book have only served to increase the historical links between the biblical family and Egypt. But in what way does this link to Egypt help in explaining away these curiously 'Judaic' names? How did Jesus' father become known as Joseph, for instance?

Joseph

The answer to this question lies in the fact that the family of Jesus travelled into Egypt, partly for his safety but perhaps more importantly for his education. If Jesus was indeed related to Cleopatra VII, then the obvious country to go to for his education would be Egypt. In fact, there may have been elements within the Egyptian priesthood who were looking for a bloodline prince of Egypt, so that the Egyptian monarchy might one day be restored.

Having found themselves in Egypt, I think it would be highly likely that this Egypto-Parthian royal family would have been given adoptive Egyptian names that reflected their positions and status. The Egyptian name given to Phraataces may well have been Joseph. While this might sound like a Judaic name, I have already argued that it was, in fact, based upon an Egyptian original. The meaning of the name Joseph (Yoseph) in Egyptian would have been *yah*  *sef*  meaning Son of the Moon. All pharaohs of Egypt were the son of one god or another, and so this name would signify the son of the Moon-god, Thoth. Another version of this same name would have been Tuthmoses, which was the same name that was given to the biblical Moses.

However, it is possible that there had been a process of feminisation going on within Egypt. The God's Wives of Upper Egypt had always been a strong faction in Egyptian royalty and theology, but the era of Akhenaton saw the role of the royal wife elevated to an equal of the pharaoh himself. This increased power of the royal wife continued into the era of the biblical United Monarchy, where the royal wife was not only very powerful, but she also became the focus of religious veneration as an incarnation of Isis. This was certainly true of the Queen of Sheba, who became the subject of veneration across Egypt, Ethiopia and the Yemen. I maintain that the Queen of Sheba was an Egypto-Judaic princess, and that she was simply following in the footsteps of Queen Hatchepsut and Queen Nefertiti in adopting the mantle of Isis.

This tradition of powerful queens continued into the Ptolemaic era, and Queen Cleopatra VII proved herself to be no less ruthless than any other monarch throughout Egyptian history in her manipulation of other monarchs in the region and in the disposing of her domestic rivals. Then we have the dramatic life-story of Thea Muse Ourania, the daughter of Cleopatra VII by Julius Caesar. She proved herself most adept at manipulating her husband, the King Phraates, and then when the time was right she murdered him and married her son instead.

Here we can see clear evidence of a line of powerful women who were effectively usurping the role of the male gods of Egypt. Traditionally in Egyptian history, we see the worship of strong male gods, who all happen to have wife goddesses who are portrayed as being in largely subordinate roles. However, the increasing power of the mother goddess, Isis, is readily apparent in the increasing prestige of the Maakare MuTamhat queens of the twentieth dynasty, whom I have linked with the biblical United Monarchy. The huge granite statue of one of these Maakare queens, which is slowly being uncovered at Bubastis in the Nile Delta, is testimony to this prestige; as is the obsessive veneration of the Queen of the Stars in the biblical book of Jeremiah.

With this ever-increasing role of the Isis queens, and the diminishing role of the traditional male deities, it is not beyond the realms of possibility that in the decades prior to the new millennium, the name Joseph now referred to a Moon-goddess rather than to the Moon-god, Thoth. The reason for thinking this is that the sister of Thea Muse was called Cleopatra Selene, or Cleopatra the Moon-goddess. Thea Muse was herself called Ourania, or the Goddess of the Heavens. Mary, the mother of Jesus was also called the Goddess of the Heavens, which is why she is often depicted as standing on the Moon and crowned with a tiara of twelve stars (see the colour section).

There is a definite possibility here that when Phraataces went to Egypt he was known there as the Son of the Moon-goddess (the son of Thea Muse Selene). In the Egyptian, this appellation would have been pronounced as Joseph 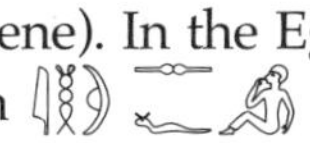 , and so this became Phraataces' common name.

Jesus

If the name Joseph can be seen to have been derived from an Egyptian title, then so can the name Jesus. It is traditionally thought that the Greek name Jesus ιησους was derived from the Hebrew name Joshua יהושע. But the Hebrew name is actually pronounced as Yehoshuah, and so the similarity between these names looks a little contrived. However, there is an Egypto-Greek alternative that seems much more reasonable.

The Egyptian name for Isis was Ast or Est  , but when the Greeks got hold of this name they transposed it into Isidos Ισιδος, with the Egyptian 't' being transliterated into a 'd' (a common transposition). Subsequently, all that has happened in later eras is that the 'd' consonant has been dropped from this name, as has happened to the English version, giving the name Isios or Isis. While this may not sound too much like the English name 'Jesus', the original Greek name for Jesus was actually pronounced as Yeaysoos or Ieysoos and so these two names are virtually identical.

However, this argument can be taken one step further, because there is actually another version of Jesus' name in the New Testament. In the book *Jesus*, I pondered over the brother of Jesus called Joses (Ieoses), for he does not seem to have any role within the family. However, this may be due to the fact that Joses is another variant of the name Jesus. The eminent theologian Robert Eisenman says of this character:

> Moreover, this is borne home by looking at the form of the two words in Greek, Ioses and Iesus. What becomes immediately apparent is that these are the same name ... The fourth brother is simply Iesos or Jesus himself! [2]

In other words, when asked to give the names of the sons of Mary, the New Testament authors simply listed them all, and not just those in addition to Jesus (which is how the verse initially reads in Math 13:55). But if 'brother' Joses was actually another name for Jesus himself, then it is apparent that his name can be spelt as either Iesus ιησους (Eeaysoos) or Ioses ιωσης (Eeoses). The latter, I think you will find, is almost an exact duplication of the Anglicised name for Isis ισιος (Eeseos).

Jesus would not, of course, simply have been named as the feminine 'Isis'; rather, his original title would have been Ben-Jesus, meaning the Son of Isis. As in the case of Joseph, as just explained, the matrilineal name may have become more important that the patrilineal. The children of Cleopatra Selene of Mauretania (Thea Muse's sister) seem to confirm this new trend, as both of these children were named after Selene's family rather than her husband's.

Had Jesus been a son of Julia Ourania, Thea Muse Ourania's daughter, and had the ancient traditions swung far enough away from the usual Egyptian male dominance, then Jesus would naturally have been called the Son of Isis. Cleopatra VII was considered to be a manifestation of Isis, and since her daughter and granddaughter were both called Ourania, they too were being identified with Isis. As I have already demonstrated in the book *Solomon,* Mary, the mother of Jesus, held the title of Handmaiden of God and Virgin, which were the two primary titles of the Egyptian God's Wife. In turn, the God's Wives, in their bare-breasted portrayals, were also closely associated with the goddess Isis. In the circumstances, it is not so surprising that a son of Julia Ourania became known as Ben Eeoses (Jesus) – the Son of Isis.

James

Once more, we tend to just assume that this is a Judaic name, but it is not. Curiously, the name 'James' is a very badly translated rendition of the Greek name Jakobos (Yakobos) Ιακωβος, which comes directly from the Hebrew Jacob (Yakob) יעקב. While the name Jacob may again seem to be a Judaic name with a long and illustrious ancestry, it is not. The name was originally Egyptian, and it was used by some of the fifteenth dynasty pharaohs of Egypt. These were the Hyksos pharaohs of Lower Egypt, and this was one of the primary reasons for my arguing that the Israelite patriarchs of the Old Testament were actually the Hyksos pharaohs of Egypt, and that the Israelite exodus out of Egypt was actually the historically attested Hyksos exodus out of Egypt.

There are two spellings of the Egyptian Jacob (Yakob) and these are  and , but the meaning of this name is highly uncertain. Since the Bible maintains that Jacob's ancestors came from the east, it may well be that this is a transliteration of a foreign name, just as the Egyptian name Cleopatra is a transliteration of the Greek title 'Muse Cleo Patra', meaning 'My Father's Glory' or even 'Heavenly Muse of my Father'. However, as I have previously argued that the biblical Hyksos-Israelites had always been resident in the Nile Delta, a possible Egyptian translation for the name 'Yakob' is *yakob*  meaning 'weep' or perhaps *yakob* 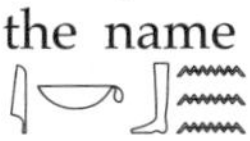 meaning 'Nile flood'. In effect, both of these names refer to life-giving rain or irrigation of the Nile Delta. Egypt could not exist without the Nile floods, and so a king who could guarantee the flood would be considered to be very powerful indeed. Since one of the pharaohs of the sixteenth dynasty was called Yacobam 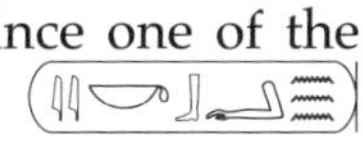, this tentative explanation may be entirely correct. In the book *Jesus* I did argue that the 'm' 'water' glyph at the end of this name was in fact a determinative glyph, which would render the true pronunciation as being Yacob (Jacob), and the meaning as being 'I am the Nile Flood'.

Judas

The Greek name Judas (Eeudas) Ιουδας comes from the Hebrew Judah (Yehudah) יהודה. Again this might sound like a typical Judaic name – indeed, the foundation for the title of the Judaic people – however, this name is again most probably of Egyptian origin. It is likely that this name stems from the Egyptian *yehudjah*  meaning 'Seed of the Moon-god' or, in other words, the 'Son of Thoth'. Again there seems to have been a great emphasis here with the Moon-gods, although in this case the deity involved is the male aspect of the Moon and so an equally valid version of this name would have been Tuthmoses.*

* Note also that the disciples had the Sicarii dagger men among their number, which is why Judas was also called Iscariot. The function of the Sicarii was the same as the later sect of Assassins, and yet there may be a link here. The Assassins are said to have derived their name from the Hashashin, a part of the Ismaili sect of Islam who were well versed in political assassination. In turn, the word 'assassin' is said to have been derived from *hashish*, the drug that supposedly made these assassinations possible. However, as modern organisers of suicide mission have attested, they prefer their walking bombs to be sane and sober, rather than drugged up to the eyeballs, as they perform their foul deeds.

Since the task of the Assassins was the same as the biblical Sicarii, and their choice of weapon was similar, perhaps there is another origin for the latter's name. Josephus says of the Parthians:

> However they made a conspiracy against Orodes of the Arsacid dynasty, and slew him at a festival ... for it is the universal custom there to carry their swords with them. [JA]

It would appear that the Parthians of the Arsacid dynasty always carried swords or knives with them, as indeed some sects of Islam still do today, and that they were not above the assassination of the aristocracy. In other words, the name for the later Islamic Assassins may have been derived from the Arsacid dynasty rather than the drug *hashish*. Prince (King) Phraataces was also of the Arsacid dynasty, and so the arrival of a new sect of assassins in Judaea in this era, who were known as the Sicarii, is not so surprising.

JA. Josephus Ant 18:45

Simon

This was a very interesting and elusive name that took a great deal of tracking down and which provided a couple of competing possibilities for us to ponder upon. The usual explanation is that Simon σιμων is taken from the Hebrew name Shimown שמעון, meaning 'hear' or 'rumour'. However, that is not necessarily so and the clue to this name's true meaning lay in the alternative appellations given to this disciple called Simon [the brother of Jesus].

Firstly, it should be pointed out that while one disciple was called Simon Peter (Simon Cephas), the other was named Simon Zelotes σιμων ζηλωτης. The additional title of Zelotes refers to the fundamentalist, zealous creed of Judaism; and so the name Zelotes ζηλωτης is taken from *zelos* ζηλος and *zeo* ζεο, which are Greek terms meaning 'anger', 'rage' or 'hot' and 'boil'. It would appear that this sect was only suitable for raging adherents to the law who boiled with indignation. That the term Zelotes may have been directly related to the name Simon (Shimon) is evident from the equivalent Egyptian root word for this name, which was *shemm-t* meaning 'hot'. Thus Simon Zelotes was so-called for his being hot-tempered, or perhaps because he followed the more radical branch of Egypto-Judaism – the Zealots. However, a quote from the Nag Hammadi gospels in a later chapter will confirm that the other Simon, Simon Peter, was definitely known for being 'hot-tempered', and so the name Simon may well have been a true description of both of these disciples' characters.

That the name Simon did refer to a hot temper is also confirmed by another nickname for Simon Zelotes, which was Simon the Canaanite σιμων κανανιτης. Now the term Canaanite may seem to indicate that Simon Zelotes was a Phoenician (a Canaanite), but the biblical Concordance also links this term back to the Hebrew word *qana* קנא, which again means 'jealousy' or 'rage'. The possible roots for Simon's second name or title in Egyptian are *kena* and *qendj* , which both mean 'rage', 'anger' and 'indignation'.

However, this is not the only interpretation that can be placed upon this particular 'surname'. As well as meaning 'zealous', the root for the Greek word *canaanite* κανανιτης is the Hebrew *canaanite* כנעני, which means 'merchant', as was pointed out in the last chapter. But this word was, in turn, derived from *qana* קנא meaning 'purchase' and *kanas* כנס meaning 'gather' or 'collect'. So here we come back to the possibility that Simon Zelotes was not so much zealous for the law (of Moses) as he was for the gathering of other people's money. Even the Greek term *zelotes* ζηλωτης, Simon's more usual name, can refer to the desire to gain other people's belongings.

Thus, as has already been proposed, Simon Zelotes, the brother and disciple of Jesus, may not have been a religious fundamentalist but rather a tax collector. Since the entire dispute between Judas of Gamala and the Jerusalem authorities was over the province of Aurania's (Bethanya's) tax-free status, and Judas' refusal to pay the Romans any taxes, I personally think that the latter is more likely.

However, since the Hebrew language is directly descended from the Egyptian language, it is not so surprising that we should also find the original root of the word *qana* קנא in the Egyptian. The term was probably derived from *tennu-t* meaning 'numbers' and this was later modified into the word *tennu-t* meaning 'taxes'. The change from the Egyptian *tennu* to the Hebrew *qanna* lies well within the known variations of Egyptian pronunciation.

Mary

In the book *Jesus,* I demonstrated that the name 'Mary' possibly originated with the pharaonic title of Meri , which means 'loved by'. The name generally refers to the pharaoh being 'loved by' a particular deity, hence the common title of Meri Amun (Loved by Amun). As it happens, Queen Cleopatra VII had a very similar title, which was Neteret Merit Se , which probably means 'Goddess Loved by Father'. The 't' at the end of the words *neter-t* and *meri-t* simply confirms that the feminine aspects of god and love were being implied. In Egyptian terms, the 'father' would have related to a heavenly father, but the Greco-Egyptian meaning may have been referring to a mortal father. In many respects, this Egyptian title is a copy of the Queen's better-known Greek name, Thea Cleo Patra, which means 'Goddess Glory of Father'.

In New Testament terms, the primary character who was 'loved by god' – indeed, sufficiently loved that she became pregnant by this same god – was also called Meri. This was, of course, Mary the mother of Jesus. The proof that this Egyptian root was the true origin of this name lies in its alternative meanings and the alternative nicknames that were given to Mary herself.

Orthodox theologians would disagree with the interpretation just given and so the standard biblical Concordance gives a meaning of 'rebellion' for the name Mary, which is hardly suitable as the name for a young lady. As ever, this translation was probably made to draw people away from the true meaning, which has more to do with pharaonic titles than a rebellious child. But this is not the only orthodox interpretation, and St Jerome gave the following alternative:

> One of the meanings assigned to the name Mary in Martianay's edition of St Jerome's works is *pikra thalassa* or *bitter sea.* Owing to the corrupt condition in which St Jerome found the 'Onomastica' of Philo and of Origen, which he in a way re-edited, it is hard to say whether the interpretation 'bitter sea' is really due to either of these two authorities; at any rate, it is based on the assumption that the name *miryam* is composed of the Hebrew words *mar* (bitter) and *yam* (sea). [3]

So the name for Mary may have been derived from the Hebrew *meri-yam* ים מרי meaning 'bitter sea', which was obviously a reference to either the Dead Sea or the Mediterranean. In fact, it is most likely to have been a reference to the latter, because this term is not Hebrew, but Egyptian. The most obvious alternative to the Egyptian *meri* is the word *mer* , which refers to a body of water of any size, or perhaps *merii-t* meaning a 'sea'. In a similar fashion, the Egyptian equivalent of *yam* ים is *yam* or *yama* meaning 'sea'. Thus, in the Egyptian, the name Meri-yam (Miriam) referred to the Sea-Sea or the Great Sea, which was indeed a reference to the Mediterranean. The Hebrew language has taken this original root and translated it as the Bitter-Sea, and this again refers to the Mediterranean.

However, having said all this I still do not believe that 'Mediterranean' is a suitable name for a young child, let alone a princess. It is always possible that this translation was derived in the first century AD, because of Mary's (probably Mary Magdalene's) well-known journey with her daughter Sarah across the Mediterranean to southern France. Alternatively, this name may be an oblique reference to the celestial seas, over which the great barque of Aton-Ra sailed. In which case, Mary may have been associated with the sky-goddess, Nut.

Certainly, the name Mary, or Miriam in the Hebrew, is not a first century invention, for the sister of Moses was also called Miriam. But Moses was an Egyptian prince, even by the admission of the Christian priesthood, thus even the Catholic Encyclopaedia wonders if the name for Mary was originally Egyptian. Indeed it was – but a reference to a sea was not a typical Egyptian appellation or title for a princess.

The outcome of all this deliberation is that the name Mary is highly unlikely to have meant 'rebellion' and it is almost as unlikely to have originally meant 'sea'. But the fact that the phonemes for her name work best in the original Egyptian demonstrates that this was originally an Egyptian name, and thus the most apt and historically attested meaning of the name is the standard pharaonic title Meri , meaning 'loved by'. However, just as in the case of Cleopatra's name, this name can refer to the person being loved by the gods or the lady in question being a love goddess herself; and the latter interpretation links Mary with Isis, Astarte and Aphrodite once more. Since I have already demonstrated, in the book *Solomon,* that Mary was following in the footsteps of the Maakhah Tamar queens in being a God's Wife, her direct association with Isis and Aphrodite is assured: for the God's Wives were indeed 'Love Goddesses'. In fact, perhaps a better term would actually be 'Sex Goddesses', for the primary duty of the God's Wife was to caress god's penis and allow him to ejaculate.

This epigraphic evidence for Mary's title's direct descent from the Maakhah Tamar queens of Egypt (and the United Monarchy of Israel) underlines Mary's Egyptian heritage once more, undermining any politically correct moves to turn Mary into a negress. Once again, this analysis demonstrates that the name Mary was not Greek, nor indeed was it Hebrew. In fact, the name 'Mary' is pure Egyptian, and so it should not be so surprising that both Thea Muse Ourania and her daughter Julia Muse Ourania became known as Mary.

Talmud

The names that have just been explored are those contained within the biblical accounts. However, the Judaic Talmud gives us an alternative point of view and some very different names for the same characters in this saga, and this gives us a second opportunity to see the true ancestry of the biblical family.

One of the more famous names from the Talmud is that of Pantera, who was reputed to have been the father of Jesus. It has already been demonstrated in the book *Jesus,* that the name Pantera was probably derived from the Egyptian title of Pa-neter-Ra  meaning 'Belonging to the God Ra' or even 'My God Ra'. However, following on from this extensive research, it is now possible that we can gain a more comprehensive translation of this name. The full quote from the Babylonian Talmud is as follows:

> 'He who cuts upon his flesh'. It is tradition that Rabbi Eliezer said to the wise, 'Did not Ben Stada bring spells from Egypt in a cut upon his flesh?' They said to him 'He was a fool, and they do not bring proof from a fool'. (Ben Stada is Ben Pandira. Rab Chisda said 'The husband was Stada, the paramour was Pandera'. The husband was Pappos ben Jehudah, the mother was Stada. The mother was Miriam, the dresser of women's hair; as we say in Pumbeditha 'Such a one has been false to her husband')'. (Original brackets) [T4]

The first thing that is abundantly clear from this quote is that the authors of the Talmud knew an awful lot more than they were giving away in their vast biblical commentary, and that their first and foremost objective was to conceal the truth from all but a select few of Judaic initiates.

That this is a fact can be demonstrated by the term 'the mother was Miriam, the dresser of women's hair'. This phrase has been derived from '*Miriam magaddela nashaia*' (or *Miriam magbalah nesaiyr* מרים מגבלה נזיר) meaning 'Miriam the hair dresser'. But if the phrase is read once more, it is apparent that this is simply an obvious play on words for 'Miriam Magdalene Nazarene', or 'Mary Magdalene the Nazarene'. Note here that *nesaiyr* נזיר does indeed also mean Nazarene, and so Mary Magdalene is simply being given the same title as Jesus. The only possible reason for this wordplay has to involve a deliberate cover-up of the characters being discussed.

As has been mentioned by many commentators, Jesus was not 'of Nazareth', for the town did not exist at this time; instead, he was 'the Nazarene'. The term 'Nazarene' actually refers to a 'fish', a sign that became the icon of early Christians and referred to the astrological sign of Pisces. This quote is, therefore, seeming to identify Mary Magdalene as the mother of Jesus, but in fact this jump in the generations is not the problem it may initially seem. The terms 'Magdalene' and 'Nazarene' are both formal titles, and it is likely that Mary the Virgin was also called 'Magdalene', as I have suggested in the book *Solomon*.

Incidentally, it is from this 'dresser of hair' pun that a famous children's story was derived. The name Magdalene is derived from the Hebrew *magdalah* מגדלה meaning 'tower', which was in turn derived from the Egyptian *maktar* or *maktal* , which again means 'tower'. The tower in question was actually a phallic symbol, but that is immaterial in this instance. The point of interest here is the linking of the princess who was known for both her hair and a tower, and the result was the ingenious fairy-story known as Rapunzel. The Catholic Church could persecute people for many perceived transgressions of Church doctrine, but writing children's fairy-stories was not high on the list – hence the Illuminati's dependence on tales such as Cinderella, Sleeping Beauty and Rapunzel. [5]

Following that short digression, it can be seen that the rest of the quote from the Babylonian Talmud is similarly and deliberately confusing in the extreme, and so it may be worth our while dissecting it piece by piece, as there is a wealth of information to be found within its convoluted and secretive folds. Firstly, it should be noted that this quote emanates from the time of Rabbi Eliezer who was a disciple of R. ben Zaccai, who died in old age some time before AD 80. Since I maintain that Jesus died in AD 70 during the siege of Jerusalem, it is likely that Zaccai knew of Jesus, or at the very least was contemporary to all of the events of the New Testament.

In the quote above, the comments of Zaccai or Eliezer are the first elements within quotation marks, while the bracketed comments are the observations of the Judaic Babylonian school of Pumbeditha.* The comments of Zaccai indicate that Ben Stada (the son of Stada) brought spells from Egypt in a flesh-wound, a term that has been interpreted within the Judaean Gemara as a tattoo. However, masonic ritual would suggest that this was indeed a cut in the flesh rather than a skin marking.** The bracketed comments about this statement firstly demonstrate that Ben Stada and Ben Pandira were the same individual (the mother may have been Stada while the father may have been Pandera). The third contention, by Rab Chisda, was that Stada and Pandira were both men – one the husband and the other the secret lover of Miriam Stada (Mary the Virgin). However, since Mary was called Stada, the latter assertion would seem unlikely.

The confusion between Stada and Pandira may have arisen because the title Pandira can be associated with a god. Since Mary and all the queens of Egypt were impregnated both by their husbands and by the gods, the wives of the pharaohs had both mortal husbands and heavenly lovers. In this case, the paramour (or lover) idea may have referred to a god. However, the correction to this statement is that Stada was indeed the mother and the father now gains another name – that of Papos of the Jews. The following table may clarify this situation.

Husband	**Wife**	**Son**
Pandira	Stada	Ben Pandira (Son of Pandira)
Papos	Hair dresser	Ben Stada (Son of Stada)

So it would appear that the names Ben Stada and Ben Pandira can be directly associated with Jesus within the Judaic traditions in the Talmud, and so the names Stada and Pandira have to be directly associated with the parents of Jesus. But if this is so, then how can these names be similarly associated with the family of Thea Muse and Julia Ourania?

* Pumbeditha was one of the great Central Asian Jewish colleges, of which Nahaiclea and Sora were two others. The version of the Pentateuch known as the Okelos of Babylon emanated from Pumbeditha and was also accepted as authoritative in Judaea.

** Some masonic sects still cut the flesh on their legs or lower backs in recognition of this age-old tradition.

V *Judaic Names?*

Stada

It has been suggested that the term Stada originated from the Aramaic *satat da*, meaning 'gone astray', which may have been a reference to the quote saying that Miriam had had a paramour or lover. However, since all the other names from the biblical family have had Egyptian origins, perhaps this name does too. If this were the case, then the obvious derivation would be *stata*  meaning 'archer'.

Now while the meaning of this term may not have been immediately obvious to classical theologians, it does become more apparent when studying the history of Parthia and the numismatics or coins of this era. As it happens, the Arsacid dynasty of Parthia was carved out and created by forces of mounted archers, and so nearly all of the coins of Parthia show the monarch on the obverse of the coin, while the reverse displays the image of an archer. It was from this archer symbology that the Parthian princely title of Tiridates was coined. Remember also that Zamaris, the Babylonian Jew who fled to Judaeo-Syria, and who may well have founded the city of Umm el-Jimal, had with him 500 mounted archers. In terms of this new interpretation of the biblical family, Jesus would indeed have been the 'Son of the Archer', the son of a Parthian princess or queen.

Pandira

It has long been thought that the name Pandira was derived from the Latin *pantera* meaning 'panther', and so some historians have sought to associate this title with a Roman legionary of the same name. This suggestion gained added impetus when a first century tombstone was discovered in Bingerbruck, Germany, which has an inscription that reads: 'Tiberius Julius Abdes Pantera of Sidon, aged 62, a soldier of 40 years service, of the 1st cohort of archers, lies here.' That Jesus was descended from a Roman legionary may have been a reasonable assumption for the theological fraternity – who continually try to promote the poor carpenter story and thereby undermine Jesus' royal heritage – but if Jesus was the 'King of the Jews' then it is more than likely that he had parents of royal blood on both sides. So is there an alternative rendering for the name 'Pandira'?

Although we do not have a comprehensive history of the events and marriages within Thea Muse Ourania's family, we do have a strong suspicion that her daughter, Julia Ourania, married Ptolemy of Mauretania. (See the family tree in the appendix.) Ptolemy was also a direct descendant of Cleopatra VII, and therefore he was Julia's cousin (their mothers being sisters). Since Ptolemy of Mauretania was the grandson of Cleopatra VII, this marriage was a strategic move that linked Parthia and Libya in a strong dynastic alliance that may not have been greatly approved by Rome.

Since we are looking at alternative names, however, it is worth noting that Cleopatra Selene was obviously the dominant partner in her marriage with Jubba II, at least as far as the naming of their offspring was concerned. Thus it is likely that Ptolemy of Mauretania's full list of titles conformed to the traditional Egyptian Ptolemaic family format. These titles generally included the titles Ieun-Paneter Setepen-Ptah Ir-Maat-en-Ra, or various similar permutations on this theme. The meaning of these titles is something like 'Heir of the God, Chosen of Ptah, Carrying out the laws of Ra'. However, the second title could also infer 'Carpenter of Ptah', which is a familiar title in regard to biblical research.

The first part of this title is also interesting, as the slightly different cartouche of Ptolemy VIII demonstrates that the god in question was Ra and this would result in a title that was pronounced as Ieun-Paneter-Ra instead (the word Paneter is often transliterated as Panedjer). Note that the scribes have positioned both god-flags (neter or nedjer) as facing the god image (Ra), as a mark of respect to the Ra glyph, even though this represents a contravention of the normal rules. But this title gives us an interesting possibility, for if one were simply reading the cartouche from left to right, and ignoring the usual Egyptian conventions regarding the positioning of god-names, the title actually reads as Panter-Ra-Ieun (Pandjer-Ra-Ieun) meaning 'I am Ra's Heir'. Thus if a scribe had access to the cartouche of a Ptolemy and read from left to right, they would read off the title P.a.n.dj.e.r.R.a, or Pandera. Here is the full reasoning for the Talmudic assertion that the father of Jesus was called Pandera.

Fig 33. A generic cartouche of a Ptolemy PanterRa-Ieun Setepen-Ptah Irmaat, pharaoh of Egypt.

About twenty years ago, the author Ahmed Osman [6] determined that Panedjer-Ra referred to the god Ra, which was a revelation in itself, but here we find that PanderRa was used as a formal title by the Ptolemaic dynasty of Egyptian royalty, and that this royal line may well have been the direct ancestor of Jesus (through Thea Muse). This association between the father of Jesus and the god Ra would also explain why the Bible says that Jesus' grandfather was called Helios. The Greek Helios and the Egyptian Ra are, after all, the same deity.

In fact, one can take this argument one stage further in its associations with Jesus, because the full title of Caesarion Ptolemy XV, the son of Cleopatra and Julius Caesar, was (reading phonetically) Pandjer-Ra-Ieun Nehem . The final addition to this tile means 'saves', or perhaps more accurately 'saves by water'. Thus Ben Pandira was also the Saviour, as was Jesus himself. In fact, Caesarion would appear to have been the only Ptolemy to have adopted this title. But if Ptolemy of Mauretania, who was the nephew of Caesarion, was inheriting the latter's titles, then he too would have been titled 'Saviour' and may well have passed this title on to his children. Taking all of this into account, the full list of Jesus' titles would have been:

Egyptian title	**Biblical title**
Setepen Ptah	God's Carpenter
Nehem	Saviour
Ieun Pander Ra	Only Begotten Son (God's heir)
Irmaat Ra	Mediator (God's Judge)

Here, then, we have the intriguing possibility that Jesus was the son of Ptolemy of Mauretania and Julia Ourania. But if this was so, then this would have been another mighty threat to Augustus' leadership of the Roman Empire. In this case, Jesus would have been a direct descendant of the previous emperors and monarchs of Rome, Egypt, North Africa and Parthia; and this would mean that with enough public support, Jesus could have united all of the primary empires of this era. At one stroke, Ptolemy and Julia Ourania could have become king and queen of a united Romo-Egypto-Parthian empire that encompassed nearly all of the known world – and established the most powerful dynasty the world had ever seen. Since the birth of such a well-connected prince to such illustrious parents would have been a grave threat to the reign of Emperor Augustus and King Artabanus II of Parthia, the opposition to Jesus' birth may not simply have come from Herod and the Jerusalem rabbis.

One thing is certain, and that is that the Judaic rabbis knew of Jesus' royal heritage, but chose to deliberately conceal it within convoluted tales and Hebrewised transliterations of Egyptian titles. To have announced to the world that Jesus was descended from Egyptian, Roman and Parthian royalty would have demonstrated that Judaism has a very close relationship with Egyptian theology, and this they could not allow. Instead, in an unlikely collusion between the Judaic rabbis and Saul-Josephus' deliberately vague New Testament accounts, no effort was spared in distancing Jesus and his family from their royal Egyptian and Parthian roots. However, what this process of obfuscation has left us with is a trail of clues that will eventually lead us back to the hidden truth.

VI

Revised Testament

The evidence shown so far strongly suggests that the biblical family was descended in some manner from the Egypto-Parthian family of Thea Muse Ourania. But a cursory glance at the New Testament accounts will not support that hypothesis in any way, for there does not appear to be any mention of either Persia or Parthia in relation to the biblical family. So how can this be so? If Jesus was descended from Thea Muse, then how was the Egyptian and Egypto-Persian ancestry and culture of the biblical family masked so comprehensively? And, if it has indeed been covered up so successfully, one might also ask how this new theory can ever progress beyond being an unsubstantiated conjecture – for there appears to be no conclusive evidence for this theory within the biblical texts.

However, there may well be a method of seeing through this veil of biblical obfuscation. The first thing to note is that it is highly likely that all of the biblical texts came though the offices of Saul-Josephus, the first century's premier theologian and historian. Although Saul-Josephus was highly prolific in his writing and mostly highly accurate in his endeavours, he was no impartial bystander in this drama. Firstly, Saul-Josephus' historical work had to fit into the Roman perspective of Judaea, for the Romans were his patrons and they expected (on pain of exile or death) that Rome would be portrayed in a favourable light. Secondly, Saul-Josephus had serious opposition to his proto-Christian works, both from traditional Jews and also from the Church of Jesus and James: the 'fourth creed' of Judaeo-Israel.

Saul-Josephus' new creed (the fifth way) upset both traditional Judaism and the fourth creed of Jesus and James because it had been opened up to the Goyim – the Gentiles or non-Jews. Saul-Josephus could see that there were more Gentiles in the world than Jews, and if a religion was going to become powerful and influential, it should play to the largest audience. In addition, Judaism was a rigorous religion to follow, while the fourth creed's masonic-style initiatory system meant that only a few selected candidates were accepted. Saul-Josephus saw that the ideal religion allowed anyone in, as long as they put money in the collecting plate. This was the same thought process that eventually initiated the corrupt system of indulgences, or absolution from sin by bribing god, which was nevertheless a reliable road to riches and power.

These tactics worked just as planned, and the Church of Saul-Josephus soon outstripped the parent Judaic belief systems in both influence and resources. In following this strategy, Saul-Josephus also upset the Church of Jesus and James, with his gross distortions of their doctrines. If the Church of Jesus was indeed based upon the Church of Judas of Gamala, it would seem that this sect were primarily libertarians; that is, believers in freedom of thought, expression and will, and also freedom from authoritarian controls and restrictions. As Saul-Josephus says of this 'fourth sect' of Judaism:

> ... they have an inviolable attachment to liberty, and say that god is to be their only ruler or lord. [J1]

In other words, the fourth creed were probably the ancestors of modern Masons. While Masonry has come under attack on many occasions, including from myself, for its policy of nepotism, it is also true that Masonry has attempted to guide Western civilisation away from a state of religious tyranny and towards a society of secular freedoms. The Protestant revolution and the Enlightenment era were both inspired by the Craft, and both resulted in freedoms that society had not experienced for a thousand years or more. The French and American Revolutions were also masonic revolutions, and while these events may have been repressive and bloody in themselves, in each case the goal and the eventual end result was a secular, republican nation guided by the tenets of Liberty, Equality and Fraternity.

This rallying cry to the French Revolution was a masonic phrase long before the revolution began and it underscores many of the aims and goals of Masonry. Liberty: that people should be free from tyranny. Equality: that slavery should be outlawed and all should have an equal chance to progress up the rungs of society. Fraternity: that we should treat our fellow man like a brother, and not an alien or enemy.

Not explicitly included in these three watchwords of Masonry is another basic tenet of the Craft – freedom of religion. As far as Masonry is concerned, while you are supposed to believe in a supreme being, the manner in which you conduct that belief system is up to you. There are no rigid theological doctrines to follow within Masonry, which is why both the French and American constitutions outlawed all religion within the state system. All state functions, from the education system to the courts of law, are supposed to be completely free from religious influences – because religion is supposed to be a personal relationship between an individual and his or her god. As Jesus said:

> And when thou prayest, thou shalt not be as the hypocrites are: for they love to pray standing in the synagogues and in the corners of the streets, that they may be seen of men. Verily I say unto you, They have their reward. But thou, when thou prayest, enter into thy closet, and when thou hast shut thy door, pray to thy Father which is in secret; and thy Father which seeth in secret shall reward thee openly. [B2]

In other words, within the Church of Jesus, the 'fourth creed' of Judaism, there was no need for an oppressive priestly hierarchy and a church in every village keeping a watchful eye on its flock. There would be a great temple for the professional theologians, as was the case in Egypt and the early years of Judaism, but for the common man religion was a private affair. These republican, masonic ethics are the reason why Jesus, Napoleon and George Washington all refused the kingship of their nations, although it was offered to each of them:

> And Pilate asked (Jesus), Art thou the King of the Jews? And he answering said unto him, Thou sayest it ... [B3]

> Pilate answered them, saying, Will ye that I release unto you the King of the Jews? ... And Pilate answered and said again unto them, What will ye then that I shall do unto him whom ye call the King of the Jews. [B4]

Unlike Jesus and James, Saul-Josephus was not interested in Liberty, Equality and Fraternity, nor was he interested in governing the people wisely and allowing freedom of religion. What Saul-Josephus wanted – and every Church that followed the 'Christian' Church of Saul has wanted ever since – was power and money. Thus the new sect of Christianity was set up with a despotic pseudo-monarch in control of a centralised pyramid of power, and this is what we see today in the Catholic Church and its pope-king. So Saul-Josephus may have used Jesus as an icon for his new Church, but in no way did the fantasy story and the Christian Church that he created reflect the true life of Jesus.

Monarch or republican?

However, if Jesus was indeed descended from the Egypto-Parthian royal family of Thea Muse, it might be countered that Jesus could not simultaneously be masonic, libertarian and republican. This might appear so, but this contradiction may be solved by looking at the evolution of libertarianism and republicanism, for each and every one of these ideals contains its own set of internal contradictions; just as the 'freedom' and 'brotherhood' of Communism was created and maintained by the tyranny of the USSR and the NKVD, Stalin's secret police.

I have a feeling that this kind of libertarianism movement was originally instituted by Pharaoh Akhenaton who, despite his despotic control over the army and the state religion, was decidedly liberal in many other respects. Within the tight straightjacket of his new religion and police-state, Akhenaton allowed many freedoms which allowed a blossoming of new modes of thought and artistic expression that had been unheard of in Egypt for thousands of years. Akhenaton was also so happy – as he and Nefertiti strolled naked around their liberal 'Garden of Eden' [Garden of Aten] in Amarna, like the ancestors of the 1960s hippy movement – that he became distinctly relaxed about his international policy; with the result that vassal states defected and chaos descended upon his borders. Akhenaton may not have been a republican in the true sense of the word, but he was distinctly liberal in many other respects and probably did think he was doing his utmost for the people, rather than the best for himself.

This form of limited liberalism may well have been the role-model for Thea Muse's government. As we shall see shortly, Thea Muse's administration in Parthia was boycotted by the nobility of that empire and so she and her son appealed instead directly to the common people; much as Akhenaton did with his rejection of the traditional priesthood and the creation of his own religious hierarchy. So while Akhenaton and Thea Muse were not real republicans themselves, through their concerted programme of destroying the established aristocracy and appointing a new administrative structure, everything below their status as monarch became fluid and this allowed many of the lower classes to rule instead. So these were both class revolutions, although not exactly in the same mould as the French and American Revolutions. As the ancient Egyptian texts said of an earlier class revolution, which was created during the turbulent Hyksos period:

> The grain is low, the measure is large,
> The weak-armed is strong-armed,
> One salutes him who saluted,

> I show you the undermost uppermost,
> The beggar will gain riches,
> The great will rob to live. [5]

In the first century AD it was to be Jesus who was to lead the new revolution, and this is why he became known as Jesus the Galilean, meaning 'Jesus the Revolutionary'. But the political process of Jesus' administration had moved on a great deal in the twelve or so hundred years since Akhenaton's reign, and masonic-style elections were being held in order to decide upon the new disciple to replace Judas. However, although the levels of political emancipation may initially appear to have increased, I still maintain that the majority of Jesus' disciples were his own brothers. And so, king or no king, it was still the ruling dynasty that controlled the electoral process. Of course, the same is true of modern democracies, despite the illusion that parliaments are controlled by the will of the people. America, for instance, may promote itself as being a true republican state, but it is still a handful of influential families who control the Senate and the choice of president.

So the Church of Jesus may well have been striving for liberty and freedom from doctrine, while the Church of Saul-Josephus was seeking a rigid orthodoxy, oppressive religious laws and a secret religious police-force to enforce this orthodoxy. Of course, it was Saul-Josephus who won this battle and so the Vatican, the Pope and the Inquisition were all created to control our thoughts, to reduce our freedoms and to blight our lives.

It took one and a half millennia to organise, but the Western world eventually fought off this despotic oppression during the Lutherian revolution and the Enlightenment era. However, the Islamic world has never been through this process and so it is still mired in orthodoxy, oppression and tyranny. That Western governments should invite this style of medieval religious repression back into the West – while knowing the level of oppression, tyranny and massacres of the innocents that fundamentalist religions have caused in previous eras – is a grave dereliction of their duty to protect our freedoms and lives bordering on treason. We allow them to continue doing so at our peril.

For Saul-Josephus, back in the first century AD, this difference in doctrine and outlook was probably enough reason to reject and oppress Jesus and Mary Magdalene and the Church they led. But there was another, more important reason for altering the texts of the New Testament in order to excise all references to Thea Muse Ourania and Phraataces, and also those that mentioned Egypt and Parthia. Jesus and Mary Magdalene were descended from the liberal and perhaps slightly hedonistic court of Thea Muse, while Saul-Josephus was a forerunner of the fire-and-brimstone Catholic Church or, indeed, the Puritans.

Similarly, Thea Muse was no doubt a highly independent woman in the direct mould of Cleopatra VII: a woman who was used to power, wealth, ostentatious displays and dominance, not only over the men in her court but also over the men of the priesthood and the aristocracy. Here was a woman who could murder her husband in cold blood, and marry her son in contravention of all the prevailing laws of the land. Thea Muse was obviously not a woman to be trifled with, and for the obsequious, cowardly, craven Saul-Josephus (when faced with his superiors, be they Judaic or Roman), this kind of strong-willed woman probably scared him rigid. Accordingly, when laying out the tenets of Christianity, Saul-Josephus says in his letter to Timothy:

> In like manner also, that women adorn themselves in modest apparel, with shamefacedness and sobriety; not with braided hair, or gold, or pearls, or costly array. [B6]

> But I suffer not a woman to teach, nor to usurp authority over the man, but to be in silence. [B7]

Saul-Josephus' attitude towards women was to provide a conflict of wills, a clash of titans. Whether it was his fear of women like Thea Muse or whether it was simply an opportunity to demonise Jesus and Mary Magdalene, Saul-Josephus outlawed all sexual liberalism and demoted women to the role of priestly assistants. Disgusted with the prospect of incestuous royal marriages in his own backyard, Saul's new sect was to be a Church with strict rules on sexual union and perhaps even a dislike of the whole concept of sex and reproduction. (See the book *Solomon* for another reason for Saul's dislike of sex and reproduction.)

However, it was probably well-known in Syrio-Judaea that Thea Muse had married her son, Phraataces, and so if Jesus was indeed descended from this royal line then none of these court intrigues could be mentioned within the New Testament. The quote from the Babylonian Talmud in Chapter I clearly demonstrates that the Judaic priesthood knew that Mary Magdalene (Jesus' sister) was a royal princess and they were not above making fun of this royal association. Similarly, the Tosephta Sanhedrin says:

> Rabbi Meir used to say ... 'It is like the case of two twin brothers. One ruled over the whole world, the other took to robbery. The one who took to robbery was caught and they crucified him on a cross. And everyone who passed by said "It seems that a king is crucified." ' [T8]

The reference to a twin brother who became a revolutionary and was crucified just has to be a covert reference to Jesus and his twin brother Judas Thomas; especially as the passers-by thought that this man on the cross was a king (of the Jews). This suggestion is reinforced by the commentary on the crucifixion that is recorded in the Koran, where a similar swapping of one twin for another takes place. The Koran says:

> They declared 'We have put to death the Messiah, Jesus the son of Mary, the messenger of God.' But they did not slay him, nor did they crucify him, because he was made to resemble another for them. [K9]

The suggestion is, of course, that it was Judas the twin who was crucified, and not Jesus. Note also that this twin 'ruled over the whole world', which seems to be a reference to a worldly rather then a spiritual realm – a king rather than a prophet. If Jesus was related to Thea Muse, and thus a prince of Rome, Parthia and Egypt, he could indeed have laid claim to being the 'king of the world' – if only he could find a throne to sit on.

The reason for all this covert ecclesiastical sniggering among the Judaic priesthood, which is to be found in the Talmud, was twofold. Firstly, there was the slightly comical plight of a prince with no throne, who tried to muster support to little effect. Secondly, since the royal ancestry of Jesus' family was well known, it was also well known that this royal family had indulged in a court intrigue that included patricide and incest. The Judaic priesthood, who distanced themselves from the fourth sect of Jesus and James, may well have seen an element of humour in all this. However, the puritanical and misogynist Church of Saul-Josephus was founded upon this very same royal family, and so Saul-Josephus had to ensure that all mention of the royal court of Thea Muse and Phraataces was covered up.

One of the methods of masking that Saul-Josephus used was to give Jesus' temporal authority, as a prince of the realm, a spiritual gloss. Thus, the titles Christos and Messiah became synonymous with being anointed by god, as god's son and saviour. But in actual fact these titles referred to the 'anointed one' and they originally denoted the secular authority of an emperor or king. (According to the Gospel of Philip the anointing oil was from the olive, which was called *chrism* and from this was derived the title 'Christ'.) St Clement says of these titles:

> Just as Arsaces was the common title of the Persian king, or Caesar that of the Roman, or Pharaoh that of the Egyptian – so also Christ was the common title for the king of the Jews. [10]

Thus, Jesus the Christ was Jesus the King of the Jews [and Romans and

Parthians and Egyptians], just as the New Testament claims; but Saul-Josephus was not in a position nor in the mood to acknowledge this.

However, masking the entire truth in a historical document is not always possible, especially when the facts are well known. The alternative, as we have already seen from many of the Old Testament texts, is for certain names and locations to be discreetly altered. Change the names, even through the use of local slang and hypocorisms or nicknames, and sometimes the true nature of the events can be utterly shrouded. The only problem with this technique, of course, is that if we can learn the meaning of the slang and the nicknames, then the original historical events suddenly re-emerge from the mists of time virtually unchanged. This is what I shall be attempting in this chapter. As we shall see, the new province of Thea Muse Ourania called Aurania, which lay to the east of the river Jordan, was not censored completely from the New Testament, it was simply and subtly altered to become the 'Kingdom of Heaven'.

Pagan Judaism

Having looked at the reason why the Parthian heritage of the biblical family may have been censored, perhaps the next problem to solve is how the religion of an Egypto-Parthian family could be considered to be in any way Judaic. If the religion of Jesus was based upon Judas of Gamala's, 'fourth creed', it would indeed have been both novel and radical (a revolution or *galilee*). However, this new 'fourth creed' was also supposed to have been based on the creed of the Pharisees – in other words, it was still recognisably Judaic. So in what way was the religion of Thea Muse Ourania, an Egypto-Parthian queen, Judaic?

Actually, perhaps this question should be turned around, for the question should really be 'what exactly was Judaism in this era?' We are all probably aware of what we think Judaism is today, but my previous books have highlighted event after event which demonstrates that Judaism prior to the first century AD was a very different animal. The royal descendants of King Solomon were, for instance, discovered worshipping an erect penis; a phallic fertility symbol. This cult obviously lasted for many centuries because the prophet Jeremiah was fulminating at the Jews for venerating decorated poles. This was quite obviously a May Pole, which is another phallic fertility symbol, and this kind of May Pole dancing used to be very popular in the UK until very recently. Tree worship was also very popular within Judaism, and many a Judaic leader from Abraham through to the kings of the Babylonian exile was guilty of planting sacred groves of trees.

Idolatry was also very popular within Judaism, despite this ritual being entirely contrary to the second of the Ten Commandments. From Moses through to King Solomon, the Judaic people were always being discovered making idols – indeed, King Solomon's Temple seems to have been ornamented with lions and bulls and cherubim, and nobody seems to have minded one iota.

Similarly, the comprehensive history of Judaism provided for us by Saul-Josephus Flavius demonstrates that there was a great deal of astronomical and astrological content within traditional Judaism. The *menorah*, the Judaic seven-branched candlestick, represented the seven known planets, while the twelve loaves of bread on the table (altar) represented the signs of the zodiac – as did the twelve sons of Jacob and the twelve disciples of Jesus. The colourful coats of Joseph and the other Judaic priesthood were also explained by Saul-Josephus in graphic cosmological terms. There were also many synagogues in the third to fifth century AD Israel that had a mosaic zodiac as the primary symbol on the floor of the synagogue. This demonstrates that even in the years following the destruction of the Temple of Jerusalem by the Romans, Judaism still had elements of astrological veneration that were central to the religion. It is unfortunate that debate on the meaning and usage of these zodiacs is largely confined to academic discussion sites, rather than the public arena, Indeed, it is noteworthy that the best analysis I could find of these Jewish zodiacs was written by a Chinese professor from Changchun University in China!

> Our goal is to show that ancient Jews used astrology in much the same way as their neighbors in Palmyra or Nabataea. The Jewish variety of astrology, in turn, will help explain the famous zodiac mosaics. A zodiac in a synagogue meant the same thing as it meant in a temple: it was a symbol of the Supreme Deity, Who ran the universe by the laws of astrology. It is important to emphasize this, for some major scholars of ancient synagogues deny that the ancient Jews did anything as irrational as practice astrology ... In this chapter and the following one, we will show that ancient Jews used astrology in the same ways as their fellow Syrians. [12]

This again demonstrates the ease with which the academic and theological elite can effectively censor the truth about history or a religion. There is no official censorship, as such, but the discussions are rarified and confined to a small academic clique, and so the wider public knows nothing of the true history of their religion. So far, six ancient synagogue mosaics containing images of the zodiac have been discovered in Israel. These pavements date from the third to the sixth century AD and include Hammat Tiberias, Beit

Alpha, Huseifa, Susiya, Naaran, and the recently discovered mosaic at Sepphoris. The Naaran zodiac is described by Dr Ness as being:

> ... a large square, 4.05 meters on a side, containing two concentric circles, 1.6 meters and 3.5 meters in diameter, respectively. The corners hold female figures. They are damaged, but Hebrew labels tell us that they represent the four seasons. Each season was named for one of the Jewish months it contained. Summer is *tebet*, for example. The seasons are also marked with appropriate symbols. Spring, for example, has a bird and tree, while autumn has a star, perhaps for Sirius, the Dog-star, which appears in the autumn.
>
> The space between the two circles is divided into twelve wedges, each just over a meter long. Each held a figure for one of the signs as well as a label in Hebrew. The signs run clockwise, while the seasons run counterclockwise. The signs are not aligned with the proper seasons. Spring, for example, is next to Libra and Virgo, rather than Aries or another of the spring signs. The figures are badly damaged, but they seem to follow the usual Greek iconography of the signs.
>
> The center circle holds a picture of Sol Invictus, the deified sun, driving a four-horse chariot. Two horses are on either side of the chariot. He wears a cloak with stars, a crown of rays, and holds a whip. His face is gouged out, as are those of the horses. [13]

The fact that the seasons are not aligned with the astrological constellations is interesting, and there are two possible reasons for this. Firstly, these zodiacs could be displaying the Egyptian rather than the Syrio-Judaean seasons. The growing season in Egypt was known as *peret,* and this started in October or November, rather than March or April. These Egyptian springtime months coincide with the constellations of Libra and Virgo, just as they do in the Israelite zodiacs, and so this may again point towards an Egyptian ancestry for Judaism.

Alternatively, these zodiacs may have been displaying the millennial precession of the equinox, which I have described in my other works; especially since the seasons are running counterclockwise, as they do in precession. If this is so, then these zodiacs may be designed to show a particular era in history (or in the future). The current zodiac in use in all Western newspapers is significantly out of date as it shows a vernal equinox (March 21st) between the constellations of Aries and Pisces. This means that the 'modern' zodiac has not been updated since the time of Jesus. If these Israelite zodiacs were displaying the usual Western seasons, rather than an Egyptian one, then they are showing a calendar that is 210 precessional degrees, or 15,000 years, before the present time. For the reasons why this era should have been highlighted in this manner, I might refer readers to my book *Thoth:* although it has to be said that this work is decidedly more esoteric than my usual analyses of history.

Fig 35. Mosaic zodiac from the floor of the Hammath synagogue.

Although it may seem strange that the Jews followed astrology, they used to have yet more 'heretical' elements within their creed. The Queen of Heaven was another popular Judaic icon, as can be seen by the veneration of the Queen of Sheba (a name which means Queen of the Stars). The Queen of Sheba was obviously deified in death as being an incarnation of the Egyptian Isis (the Queen of Heaven), but her cult lasted at least until the Babylonian exile, where the prophet Jeremiah was again incandescent that the Jews were worshipping the Queen of Heaven. However, so ingrained was this Jewish cult that the people ignored Jeremiah completely. It is my belief that the exile of these people from Judaea, after the destruction of Jerusalem in 587 BC, was the basis for the emergence of the Sabean empire; and so the Sabeans, or star worshippers, venerated the Queen of Sheba (Queen of the Stars or Queen of Heaven).

There was also the cult of the temple prostitute in Israel, both male and female, and I discuss the similar role of the God's Wife or Temple Virgin at great length in the book *Solomon*. However, the fact that this position did exist in Jerusalem can be seen in the following verse:

> And he took away the male prostitutes out of the land, and removed all the idols that his fathers had made. [B14]

The king in question here was King Asa, the great grandson of King Solomon. However, if there was a pogrom against the male prostitutes at the Temple of Solomon it was obviously not very successful, because thirteen generations later we find that King Josiah has exactly the same problem:

> And he brake down the houses of the male prostitutes, that were by the house of the lord, where the women wove hangings for the sacred grove. [B15]

Note the mention of the sacred grove once more.

So, from the United Monarchy of King David and King Solomon all the way through to the Babylonian exile, the Jews were indulging in a variety of 'pagan' rites, including sacred prostitution, idolatry, astrology, mother goddess worship, tree worship and phallic worship. Bearing all of this in mind, what exactly was the creed of Judaism in the first millennium BC? How do we begin to define it? If Thea Muse of Parthia was indulging in a little phallus veneration, as she well might have been, was she not practising Judaism? If Thea Muse consulted her court astrologer, as she most probably did, was she not following the strict tenets of Judaism? If Thea Muse gave some money to the Temple of Jerusalem for the provision of temple prostitutes, was she not being a pious Jewess?

In short, it would seem that the Judaism of this era was very akin to Egyptian and Parthian belief systems, and thus Thea Muse could well have been considered to be a Jewess. But if an Egypto-Parthian queen could be seen as a Jewess, then, conversely, might not some the rituals of the 'fourth creed' appear to be rather Egypto-Parthian?

The Talmud certainly thinks so of the biblical Jesus, for as we have already seen it specifically identifies him as being an Egyptian Magi, or magician:

> 'Did not (Jesus) bring spells from Egypt in a cut upon his flesh?' They said to him 'He was a fool, and they do not bring proof from a fool'. [T16]

Likewise we have again seen evidence that Josephus Flavius also thought that Jesus was called the Egyptian False Prophet. In other words, far from her Egypto-Parthian heritage making an association between Thea Muse and Jesus utterly impossible, it would seem that it is absolutely essential for any claimant to the position of Jesus to have an Egypto-Parthian background.

Jesus was known in his own era as the 'Egyptian False Prophet', and yet when he was born he was visited by the Parthian (Persian) Magi. It is obvious, therefore, that Jesus had both Egyptian and Parthian ancestry. But Jesus was also demonstrably aristocratic, from a royal family of some nature. There was only one Egypto-Parthian royal family who was exiled to Syrio-Judaea early in the first century AD, and that was the family of Thea Muse Ourania and Phraataces. Ergo, one might say, Jesus and Mary Magdalene must have been descended in some manner from Thea Muse Ourania, the exiled queen of Parthia.

So the ancestry of Jesus may well have been through Thea Muse and thus through Cleopatra VII. However, if we look to the New Testament for an answer to the question of Jesus' ancestry, we are in for a bit of a shock. Unfortunately, the genealogies that these texts provide are entirely contradictory, and so they cannot tell us anything about Jesus' origins. However, it might be worth pointing out that within these two genealogies, the name Sadoc (Zadok) belonged to a colleague of Judas of Gamala, while Heli was the name of Cleopatra VII's son by Mark Antony.

Genealogy of Jesus according to the gospel of:

Matthew	**Luke**
Jesus	Jesus
Joseph	Joseph
Jacob	Heli
Matthan	Matthat
Eelizar	Levi
Eliud	Melchi
Achim	Janna
Sadoc	Joseph
etc:	etc:

Kingdom of Heaven

The evidence seems to suggest that the ritual and religion of early Judaism could easily have been confused with Egypto-Parthian rituals. Having said that, there still does not appear to be much, if anything, within the New Testament that can be said to directly link the biblical family with the Parthian royal family. But that may simply be because we are conditioned to these biblical events all occurring among a poor artisan's family in Judaea and Galilee, and not among the pseudo-masonic royalty of Bethanya to the east of the river Jordan.

But if we expand our horizons a little and empty our mind of preconditions, it is just possible that an alternative gospel may appear before our eyes. For example, it is said of John the Baptist:

> Verily I say unto you, among them that are born of women there hath not arisen a greater than John the Baptist: yet he that is but little in the Kingdom of Heaven is greater than he. [B17]

If we were to read this verse superficially, it would seem that John is being described as an ordinary man, for we are all born of women; and so a comparison is presumably being made between mortals and semi-divine beings like Jesus. However, the verse goes on to say that anyone who was born in the Kingdom of Heaven would be greater than John. But since Jesus was supposed to have been the unique creation of a singular god, who else in the Kingdom of Heaven could have been greater than John? The verse does not seem to make a great deal of sense, but perhaps we are not reading it correctly.

Those who have 'ears to hear' might have noticed that *gune* γυνη, the Greek term for 'woman', can also be translated as 'widow'. If the latter were the correct reading then John would have been referred to as a 'Son of a Widow', which would make his position much more clear. The term 'Son of a Widow' refers to a Mason, and since I have already demonstrated that Jesus was a Mason, this would make a great deal of sense. With this alteration, this same verse would now read as:

> Verily I say unto you, Among them that are Masons there hath not arisen a greater than John the Baptist: yet even those who are lowly in the Kingdom of Heaven are greater than he.

Contrary to the standard interpretations of the New Testament, John the Baptist actually appears to have been a leading Mason rather than a Neolithic *Stig of the Dump* character, covered in animal skins. Instead of being a humble hermit, he was probably a Past-Master in the esoteric arts and Gnostic theology (and since the Egyptian high priesthood wore the leopard skin as a mark of their high office, perhaps John did wear a few animal skins). This alternative interpretation of John's status is supported by a comment in the Clementine Recognitions, which states:

> It was at Alexandria that Simon (Magus) perfected his studies, being an adherent of John (the Baptist) ... Of all John's disciples, Simon was his favourite. [18]

Again, this verse identifies John the Baptist as being someone far removed from the hairy hermit of popular biblical mythology, for it would appear that he was an influential teacher in Alexandria, the most cosmopolitan city in the Roman empire. In addition, the term *magus* has already been explained as denoting a Parthian astrologer or councillor, one of the Magi 'wise men' who came to visit the infant Jesus. So why, in this case, was John the Baptist the tutor of a (possibly influential) Parthian (Persian) astrologer and councillor?

The answer to this can be found in the verse about John the Baptist we have just looked at. The second sentence of this verse seems to suggest that only those in the 'Kingdom of Heaven' can be greater than John the Baptist, and this is most definitely the theological interpretation of this verse that the Catholic Church would like to promote. But what does the 'Kingdom of Heaven' actually refer to? It may superficially appear to be a common biblical term that refers to the 'Kingdom of God', and not something worth exploring; but in fact this title is only used in the Gospel of Matthew, and it may well have a completely different meaning to the one normally supposed. The true interpretation of this title can be seen if we use the original Greek term for 'heaven', which is *ouranos* ουρανος. Using the original Greek term, the verse now becomes:

> Verily I say unto you, Among them that are Masons there hath not arisen a greater than John the Baptist: yet even those who are lowly in the <u>Kingdom of Ourania</u> are greater than he.

Wow! Surprising as it may seem, the true translation for Matthew's 'Kingdom of Heaven' is the 'Kingdom of Ourania', and it is highly likely that this was actually a reference to the 'Kingdom of Thea Muse Ourania', the exiled queen of Parthia.

The alternative to this title, which is used in the other gospels of the New Testament, is the 'Kingdom of God'. Again, this may seem like a spiritual abode in the heavens, but in actual fact this title is simply using the term *theos* θεος or *thea* θεα; and so the biblical 'Kingdom of God' was called the 'Kingdom of Thea'. When combining the titles of these two common biblical kingdoms, we can now derive the 'Kingdom of Thea Ourania', and this just has to be a reference to the 'Kingdom of Thea Muse Ourania'.

However, it should be remembered that we have already identified exactly where the Kingdom of Thea Muse Ourania was. This kingdom was no longer in Parthia itself, for Thea Muse and Phraataces had already been exiled from that land; instead it was a small province to the east of the river Jordan, and it was indeed called the Kingdom of Aurania, or the Kingdom of Ourania. In fact, this name is the basis of the modern name for this region, which is the Hauran.

Thus, this verse from the New Testament was intimating that John the Baptist was an influential Mason, but that those Masons who had arrived in Syrio-Judaea from Parthia were much more influential than he. Once more, this evidence suggests that Jesus was born from the royal family of Thea Muse Ourania, the queen of Parthia – and so yes, Jesus did understand himself to be of a greater social status and importance than John.

The 'Kingdom of Heaven' is mentioned numerous times within the Gospel of Matthew, so is it possible that the radical new interpretation for this title can be sustained and justified?

> Another parable put he forth unto them, saying, The Kingdom of Heaven is like to a grain of mustard seed, which a man took, and sowed in his field. Which indeed is the least of all seeds: but when it is grown, it is the greatest among herbs, and becomes a tree, so that the birds of the air come and lodge in its branches. [B19]

> Another parable he spake unto them; The Kingdom of Heaven is like unto yeast, which a woman took, and hid in three measures of meal, till the whole was leavened. All these things Jesus said unto the multitude in parables. [B22]

These parables may seem insignificant, but they both indicate that the 'Kingdom of Heaven' was quite small, and that it is destined to grow larger. Theologians will say that this parable pertains to the Church itself, and in the light of these investigations it may well refer to the 'fourth creed' of Judas, which was superseded by the Church of Saul (Christianity).

However, it is also possible that these parables refer to the Kingdom of Ourania once more. Thea Muse's empire had once encompassed all of the lands of the Parthian empire, but the royal family was now exiled in a small province called Bethanya (Aurania), located to the east of the river Jordan. The royal family had arrived in Bethanya with a hundred assorted family members and courtiers, plus a small loyal detachment from the army. The Kingdom of Ourania was most definitely a 'mustard seed', and it was desperately seeking to expand in any direction that it could. This expansion included designs on retaking Parthia, and also on the neighbouring state of Judaea itself.

But if the province of Ourania (Aurania) desired to expand then it needed manpower. The answer to this requirement was to send out the disciples, saying:

> Blessed are the poor in spirit: for theirs is the Kingdom of Heaven.

> Blessed are they which are persecuted for righteousness' sake: for theirs is the Kingdom of Heaven. [B23]

This was not a supernatural afterlife that was being offered to the huddled masses; instead, it was a life of toil in the province of Ourania (Bethanya), in return for the basics of food and shelter. Since this has been a successful ploy used by many an emerging empire, it is not so surprising that we should see its reappearance in our modern era:

> Give me your tired, your poor,
> Your huddled masses, yearning to breathe free,
> The wretched refuse of your teeming shore,
> Send these, the homeless, tempest tossed to me,
> I lift my lamp beside the golden door! [24]

As far as America was concerned, the majority of people who arrived on those shores were also 'persecuted for righteousness' sake' – oppressed by the various 'peace loving' religious sects and authorities that still stalked the European continent.

So it would seem that the New Testament disciples were looking for immigrant workers to construct their new city in Ourania. And just in case the poor, huddled masses were afraid of the long journey to the east, the disciples in Judaea also preached:

> And as ye go, preach, saying, The Kingdom of Heaven is nearby. [B25]

While this argument can hardly be construed as positive evidence that the 'Kingdom of Heaven' referred to the 'Kingdom of Ourania', there is another parable that places this interpretation beyond doubt. We shall come to this parable in a minute, but in the meantime the following verse deals with moneylending. The orthodox view is that Jesus was against moneylending and profit, but if he was a son of Judas of Gamala, the collector of the taxes in Aurania, then Jesus should have been in favour of taxation and profit. As we have seen, Jesus often met with tax collectors, but was he a capitalist too?

This is highly likely, for there is a curious parable in which an employer from the Kingdom of Ourania gives money to three of his servants and then departs on a long journey. Upon his return two of the servants had invested their money and doubled it. However, the third servant simply stored the money and just gave it back later, with no interest. At this, the employer from the Kingdom of Ourania (Aurania) had a fit of rage:

> His lord answered and said unto him, Thou wicked and slothful servant ...

> Thou oughtest to have put my money to the exchangers, and then at my coming I should have received mine own with usury (interest). Take therefore the money from him, and give it unto him which hath more money. For unto every one that hath shall be given, and he shall have abundance: but from him that hath not shall be taken away even that which he hath. [B26]

Have readers never wondered why such a strange parable was placed in the New Testament? It is not the sort of thing that gets preached much from the pulpit, is it? ('Dorothy, I would suggest that we take everything from the poor of this parish and, err, let's give it all to the wealthy.' 'Oh yes indeed, splendid idea. More tea vicar?')

This is not exactly the kind of socialist ethos that we are conditioned to expect from Jesus' teachings, but this is entirely the style of government that Judas of Gamala would have been familiar with. Judas was running an independent tax-free province, and he needed good investments to meet his expenses and pay for his standing army, which included 500 cavalry. In addition, the province of Ourania (Aurania) needed an administrative authority, which could carry out the diktats of the ruling family. This topic is also discussed in the New Testament, and the verse in question reads as:

> At the same time came the disciples unto Jesus, saying, Who is the greatest in the Kingdom of Heaven? And Jesus called a little child unto him, and set him in the midst of them. And said, Verily I say unto you, Except ye be converted, and become as little children, ye shall not enter into the Kingdom of Heaven. Whosoever therefore shall humble himself as this little child, the same is greatest in the Kingdom of Heaven. [B27]

At first reading, it might seem impossible that this statement could have anything to do with a royal court, but this is not the case as the term for 'little child' is *paidion* παιδιον, which can also be interpreted as a 'king's servant' or 'minister'. If these same verses were to be interpreted in this manner, then they could be translated as:

> At the same time the disciples came to Jesus, saying, Who is the greatest in the Kingdom of Aurania? And Jesus called a minister unto him, and set him in the midst of them. And said, Verily I say unto you, except ye be converted, and become as king's servants, ye shall not enter into the Kingdom of Aurania. Whosoever therefore shall prostrate himself as this government minister has, will be great in the Kingdom of Aurania.

In this new interpretation, Jesus is looking for chief ministers and courtiers to administer his new kingdom and budding empire. However, if this were the case then it would appear that Jesus was looking for blind loyalty to his regime and complete submission to his authority. So were Judas of Gamala and Jesus of Gamala looking for administrators to assist them with a religious movement, or were they instead looking for cravenly loyal servants and ministers in order to emulate the functioning of the great royal houses of the Parthian east?

> For there are some eunuchs, which were so born from their mother's womb: and there are some eunuchs, which were made eunuchs of men: and there be eunuchs, which have made themselves eunuchs for the Kingdom of Heaven's sake. He that is able to embrace this way of life, let him embrace it. [B28]

Again, the subject matter of this verse is rather peculiar, especially for the lowly Judaean artisan that Jesus was supposed to have been. What were the gawping ill-educated masses supposed to make of this instruction or parable? In fact, eunuchs have little or nothing to do with the Judaean royalty either, so why on Earth did the topic of eunuchs enter Jesus' conversation?

The answer is that this verse is simply a continuation of the discussion about ministers and courtiers (the 'little children') that has just been explored. The eunuch of the royal court was actually a Persian invention and the original duties of this courtier was to attend to the personal needs of the king. Because these intimate duties brought these courtiers into the king and queen's bed-chamber, it was considered prudent that castrated males should be employed, in order to reduce the number of court intrigues and eliminate the possibility of royal bastards. It was from the Greek *eune* ευνη meaning 'bed' that the term eunuch was derived. However, this intimacy with the king allowed the eunuchs to become highly influential and powerful advisers and ministers within the royal court.

The position of royal eunuch was taken to Egypt with the Persian conquest of that country, and once more the eunuchs became very influential ministers within the Egyptian court. Indeed, the eunuch Ganymedes was an adviser and general of Princess Arsinoe, Cleopatra VII's sister. As a general of the Egyptian army, Ganymedes almost captured Julius Caesar himself in the battle of Alexandria.

That Jesus was discussing the role of a eunuch with his disciples is highly illuminating. That this discussion was also combined with his request for ministers in his budding 'Kingdom of Ourania' is nothing short of astounding – for it would appear that Jesus was requesting that some of his disciples should become eunuchs in order to work in his fledgling royal court.

While none of these verses might be construed as positive proof that the 'Kingdom of Heaven' referred to the 'Kingdom of Ourania' (Aurania), the following quote is far more explicit and convincing.

> And Jesus answered and spake unto them again by parables, and said, "The Kingdom of Heaven is like unto a certain king, which made a marriage for his son. And sent forth his servants to call them that were bidden to the wedding: and they would not come."
>
> Again, he sent forth other servants, saying, "Tell them which are bidden, Behold, I have prepared my dinner: my oxen and my fatlings are killed, and all things are ready: come unto the marriage. But they made light of it, and went their ways, one to his farm, another to his merchandise. And others took the kings servants, and entreated them spitefully, and slew them."
>
> But when the king heard thereof, he was angry: and he sent forth his armies, and destroyed those murderers ... Then saith he to his servants, "The wedding is ready, but they which were bidden were not worthy. Go ye therefore into the highways, and as many as ye shall find, invite them to the marriage." So those servants went out into the highways, and gathered together all as many as they found, both bad and good: and the wedding was furnished with guests. [B29]

So what on Earth is this parable all about? The Church takes this as being a parable regarding the Church itself, with the 'king' being a reference to god and the 'son' being Jesus; while the 'marriage feast' was a reference to the Gospels, and the 'invited guests' an allusion to the common people who either accept or reject the Church. But this explanation is all a little contrived, and even if this scenario were true, upon what real events was this parable originally based? A parable only works if the common people can identify with the real social event it describes, as well as with the deeper meaning that it conceals – so who was this king whose nobles and lords refused to come to the wedding feast of his son? Whose day of betrothal turned into a riot? And why was Jesus, the supposed lowly 'carpenter', so interested in the court intrigues of royal dynasties rather than a humble village gathering?

The true answer to this conundrum lies in the fact that this royal family, whose wedding was rejected by the aristocracy of the realm, came from the Kingdom of Heaven. Again, this was not supposed to be a reference to the heavenly kingdom of the gods, but to the terrestrial Kingdom of Aurania, the Kingdom of Thea Muse Ourania. Once we understand this connection, Jesus' peculiar parable becomes fully understandable in each and every respect.

Firstly, the new interpretation of Jesus' ancestry and social standing being forged in this book would ensure that his parables naturally focused upon royalty, rather than the common people, because Jesus was a prince – a prince descended directly from the Egyptian and Persian royal lines, no less.

Secondly, we know that there *was* indeed a disputed marriage within the original Kingdom of Ourania (or Parthia), and this was the highly contentious marriage of Thea Muse Ourania and Phraataces. So despised was this royal Parthian marriage that I have no doubt that the noble guests from across the land did indeed refuse to come to the wedding feast, and it is highly likely that some used violence against the king's servants in order to vent their anger. In fact, the internal strife caused by this wedding was so divisive that the monarch and the prince, Thea Muse and Phraataces, were obliged to go into exile shortly afterwards.

A royal wedding where the honoured guests refuse to attend was hardly a common event in the ancient world, so what other royal marriage could Jesus be referring to? It is an absolute certainty that Jesus' parable must have been alluding to this contentious marriage of Thea Muse and Phraataces in Parthia; and so what we appear to have here is a great deal more information on this marriage than has been given to us by Saul-Josephus. The New Testament is indicating that because the aristocracy of Parthia refused to come to the wedding, Thea Muse and Phraataces dressed up the common people in *kaftans,* the robes that were given to people who are about to have an audience with the monarch, and used the common people as wedding guests instead.

Can you imagine such a scandal? A son of the Queen of England, for instance, getting married in St Paul's Cathedral and the entire congregation being composed of plebeians and beggars from the streets, all dressed in royal and lordly ermine. The aristocracy of the nation would, of course, have felt deeply angry and resentful. Not only had their complaints about the unconstitutional marriage been ignored by the royal family in the first place, but the lords' and nobles' positions of authority had been deliberately usurped and undermined by the common people. And the paupers of the land, all newly dressed up in as much aristocratic finery as could be found, were no doubt cocking a snoot at the nobility, who were probably protesting loudly outside the wedding hall. It is no wonder that the situation descended into chaos and conflict.

Not only were these the common people but there were also undesirables among them, and perhaps we can see in this bizarre marriage ceremony the origins of Jesus' empathy with the common people. The aristocracy opposed the marriage between Thea Muse and Phraataces, a rejection that this Egypto-Parthian royal family simply could not understand, but the common people and the criminals were quite happy to attend the wedding and pay homage to the royal family. The Parthian monarchy were, in short, appealing directly to the common people for their support, rather than using the nobility as deputies and intermediaries in the normal manner. This direct appeal to the masses was a distinctive trait of Jesus and his followers and their subsequent reputation for being revolutionaries or *galileans* may well have stemmed from this very event.

Thirdly, it might be presumed that there is a problem in this analysis, for the parable talks about a king and Thea Muse was most definitely a queen. Actually, this is not a great problem for the New Testament mentions a *basileus* βασιλευς or 'king' while, in a similar fashion, the Parthian coinage of Thea Muse calls her a *basilisses* βασιλεσσες. The similarity between these two terms makes the possibility of a transposition, by a scribe, intent on concealing the unmentionable truth, highly likely. So this wedding was not arranged for the son of the king so much as for the son of the queen, and the queen in question was Thea Muse Ourania.

Fourthly, let us briefly recap the reasons why the noble guests refused to come to the king or queen's wedding in the first place. The account by Matthew makes little comment on this refusal, but in fact the nobility were committing treason here. This was an order by the reigning monarch to attend the wedding of a prince of the realm, and the aristocracy simply refused to come *en masse*. So what made them make this bold stand against the monarch? What was so terrible about this particular marriage that they would risk their titles and perhaps their very lives by refusing to attend? As we have seen, the answer is to be found in Josephus' Antiquities, where he says of Thea Muse and Phraataces:

> (Phraataces) therefore formed a treacherous design against his father (Phraates IV), by his mother's assistance, with whom, as the report went, he had criminal sexual relations also. So he was hated for both these vices, while his subjects esteemed this wicked love of his mother to be no way inferior to his patricide; and he was by them, in a sedition, expelled out of the country before he grew too great. [J30]

This was not simply a sexual infatuation between mother and son, for the coinage of Parthia clearly demonstrates that mother and son were married as king and queen. This was the reason for the aristocracy, in the biblical parable, refusing to come to the marriage of their prince – for the prince concerned was Phraataces and he had already assisted his mother in the poisoning of his father, Phraates IV. Not only was the prince condemned for this criminal act, but he was now inviting the aristocracy to a wedding feast to celebrate his marriage to his mother. There are not many events that will trigger a revolt against a royal marriage, or that will foster treason among the aristocracy, but in Parthia this was definitely one of them. Polygamy and incest may have been *de rigueur* within the royal court of Egypt, but it most certainly was not in Parthia, and the result of this clash of customs was a short and decisive civil war and the exile of the royal family to Syrio-Judaea.

Strange as it may seem, the Gospel of Matthew contains a peculiar parable that makes very little sense in its traditional interpretation. However, if this parable is read instead as being a reliable description of the deadly intrigues that occurred within the royal Parthian court, it makes every sense. But Matthew does not just mention this contentious marriage, he places this parable in the mouth of Jesus himself, and so leads us to an inescapable conclusion. For Jesus to have been so concerned about this contentious marriage that he used it in his teachings, he must have been directly related to Queen Thea Muse Ourania and King Phraataces. In other words, Jesus was one of the royal princes of the Egypto-Parthian royal court, who were living in exile in the province of Bethanya ([Bethany] or Aurania.

But if the Kingdom of Heaven (Kingdom of Ourania) and the Kingdom of God (Kingdom of Thea) both refer to the Kingdom of Thea Muse Ourania, then perhaps we can also translate another famous title in much the same fashion. Of all Jesus' titles, perhaps the 'Son of God' is the most theologically evocative – Jesus, the son of the all-powerful deity, the saviour of mankind. However, a more direct and rational translation of this title may again be the 'Son of Thea'. [32] In other words, Jesus was not accused of being the son of a god in the biblical accounts, he was accused of being the son of Thea Muse Ourania.

Seven devils

It would seem that many of Jesus' parables and sayings were related to the Egypto-Parthian royalty of Thea Muse. In an earlier chapter it was confidently stated that Mary Magdalene was the sister-wife of Jesus, but if this were so then she too should betray some similarities to the world of an Egypto-Parthian princess. This is what we find, but again the evidence has been buried deeply within the convoluted terminology of the New Testament. Take the following verse, for instance:

> And a certain woman, which had been healed of evil spirits and infirmities,

> Mary called Magdalene, out of whom went seven devils. [B33]

> και γυναικες τινες αι ησαν τεθεραπευμεναι απο πνευματων πονηρων και ασθενειων μαρια η καλουμενη μαγδαληνη αφ ης δαιμονια επτα εξεληλυθει

The evil spirits are the *poneros pneuma* πονηρος πνευμα, or unclean winds, which the Koran has interpreted as the *jinn* or dust devils, the pocket-sized tornadoes that frequently traverse the sands of the Arabias. However, these winds do not have to be quite so large, as they can also refer to a breath from the mouth or nostrils. The term for the devils can also have another interpretation placed upon it, as the *daimonion* δαιμονιον can equally refer to a god or a goddess. Using these and other alterations, an alternative translation for this biblical verse might be:

> And a certain women, who had been healed by separation from bad breath and weakness, Mary called Magdalene, out of whom went seven goddesses.

Humorous as this verse may now seem, I don't think that it referred to halitosis; rather, these bad or evil breaths had some kind of spiritual nature to them. In the book *Eden* I noted that, like Mary Magdalene, the title of Queen Nefertiti also referred to winds or breaths, with her name even including the trachea glyph . Several suggestions were made as to why that should be, but no final conclusion was drawn at that time. However, in the Greco-Roman world of the first century AD we seem to have another famous 'princess', of possible Egypto-Parthian heritage, who is again somehow related to breaths or winds. So what does all of this mean, and why was breathing thought to be evil in some circumstances?

While I cannot be certain about this, I am sure that this verse must be an oblique reference to the Nine Muses of Greek mythology, who were minor goddesses of particular human attributes or endeavours. The number of Muses was variable and while the number finally stabilised at nine, it started at three and there may well have been just seven at some juncture. The latter figure would then complement the seven liberal arts or sciences of Masonry.

The initial three Muses were said to be Aoide (song), Melete (practice) and Mneme (memory). In later traditions these were altered and added to, to become the nine (no doubt to fall in line with the traditional *enead*, or the nine gods, of Egypt). The nine Muses were known as Calliope (poetry), Euterpe (music), Clio (history), Erato (lyrics), Melpomene (tragedy), Polyhymnia (sacred poetry), Terpsichore (dancing), Thalia (comedy) and Ourania (astronomy). In comparison, the seven liberal arts and sciences of Masonry are said to be grammar, rhetoric, logic, arithmetic, geometry, music and astronomy. Note that there is an amount of synergy between these two lists, a similarity that may become relevant to this investigation shortly.

The connection between 'bad breath' and the Muses is derived from the fact that the title 'Muse' was derived from the Greek *mousa* μουσα meaning 'song'; as the many attributes of the Muses were often formed into ballads and sung to the audience, as indeed were the great epics like the Iliad and Odyssey. It is from these lyrical Muses that we derive the English term 'music'. But, of course, a song is produced by a breath from the mouth, and so Mary Magdalene's 'bad breath' may well have referred to the Muses of Greece. While this link may seem a little tenuous, in actual fact we still use the same terminology today. The nine Muses were said to be the 'Inspirational Muses', in that their purpose was to inspire, invigorate or stimulate the mind. However, the word inspire also means to 'breathe in', a word that was taken from the Latin *spirare* meaning 'to breathe'.

So the process of education through stimulation of the mind involved breaths of air. I have no doubt that this concept was derived in some manner from the Egyptian opening of the mouth ceremony, where the deceased required their mouths opening in a special ceremony. No doubt this process allowed the *ka* and *ba*, the life and soul of the deceased, to come and go, to and from the body as they pleased. However, a simple extension of this belief-system may well have suggested to the Egyptians that the living can be 'inspired' through a similar process of breathing. So, at a simplistic level, the education of the mind involved the tutor breathing out information and knowledge, and the pupils breathing it in, and this was the reason for Mary Magdalene being associated with breaths (bad or otherwise).

This Egyptian explanation may also be the reason behind the spelling of Queen Nefertiti's name. As has already been mentioned, Nefertiti was associated in some manner with winds or breaths, but the link with the Greek Muses might suggest that this 'breathing' or 'inspiration' should include several different types of knowledge or gnosis. Perhaps this is why we find that Nefertiti's name included five tracheae glyphs – did her title therefore refer to five Egyptian Muses?

As a partial confirmation that these Egyptian tracheae glyphs were somehow related to the breaths of the Greek Muses, it is interesting to note that the Arabic *jinn* not only refers to a 'genie' but also to the 'heart'. It may be from the Arabic notion of the dust-devil being a physical humanoid entity, and therefore a genie of *Aladdin and the Lamp* fame, that the biblical notion of a wind being a spirit (a ghost) was derived. But the Arabic etymology also suggests that breaths are somehow connected with the heart, and the Egyptian *nefer* glyph appears to confirm this. For whatever reason, the Egyptians have placed the tracheae on top of a heart glyph, to form the composite *nefer* glyph; and so it seems likely that the Arabic *jinn* and the Greek *muse* were indeed related to the Egyptian *nefer* glyph and thus to Nefertiti.

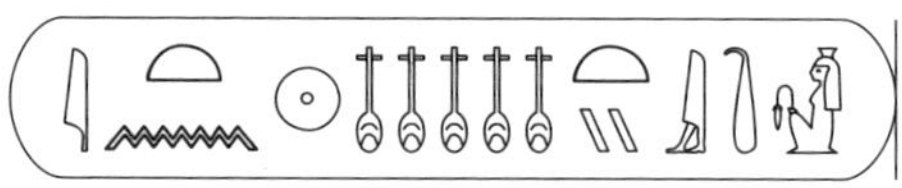

Fig 36. Cartouche of Queen Nefertiti, or perhaps Neferutiti (the plural).

Bearing in mind all of these diverse arguments, the biblical verse just quoted might now be translated as:

> And a certain women, who had been healed by separation from bad Muses and weakness, Mary called Magdalene, out of whom went the seven Muses.

I was unable to find any suitable translation for the word *poneros* meaning 'evil' and so the reason for the Muses being evil remained a mystery at this stage. So why was Mary only 'healed' when the Muses, or knowledge (gnosis), had been taken out of her? The answer to this is that we may be seeing this verse through the eyes of Saul and his despotic offspring, which is now known as the Catholic Church. I have previously argued that Saul, the founder of the Catholic Church, was not initiated into the higher degrees of the Church of Jesus and James, and so he remained ignorant and fearful of the seven sciences. This was certainly so of the later Catholic Church, which proved to be the second largest millstone around the neck of mankind's technological and educational advancement – the largest millstone being Islam.

The Dark Ages of the first millennium AD were characterised by irrationality, superstition, and theological persecution and tyranny. This was gradually replaced during the Renaissance era by a grudging tolerance of some science and rational enquiry by the all-powerful Church, but the early practitioners of alchemy and astronomy always diced with death as they probed nature for logical, rational explanations. It was not until the early eighteenth century, following the retreat of the Catholic Church in the face of the Protestant revolution in northern Europe, that the true era of the

Enlightenment arose. This was the Age of Reason, as it is sometimes known; the era of freedom from religious tyranny.

It is no coincidence that it was precisely in this era that the Masons came out of the closet and formed the United Grand Lodge of England in 1717. Their daughter institution, the Royal Society, was founded shortly afterwards and this became Britain's premier scientific institution. The Royal Society was a brave new world of enlightenment, where experiments were made and conclusions were drawn that would have warranted burning at the stake in previous centuries. It was through this process of rational enquiry that the technical and industrial revolution was born, and so we owe our present wealth and contentment to both Martin Luther and the underground stream of masonic-type institutions. However, Islam has not had its Renaissance as yet, let alone its Enlightenment, and so the fundamentalist believers of the so-called 'Religion of Peace' will no doubt be murdering freethinkers in the name of the Compassionate and Merciful for some time to come.

The early Church of Saul bore more than a passing similarity to the so-called 'Religion of Peace'. So, when looking at the position of Mary Magdalene from the perspective of Saul-Josephus and his repressive, introspective Catholic Church, perhaps the biblical verse just quoted may now make a little more sense.

The seven sciences of Masonry were evil enough, in the eyes of the Catholic Church, but perhaps the seven Muses were even worse. These were seven women (goddesses) and they were practising music and dancing, while studying history and astronomy. Indeed, one of our primary institutions for learning in the modern era is the museum, which literally means the 'House of the Muses', the house where one was free to indulge in the liberal arts and even the sciences. The famous Museum of Alexandria was constructed by Ptolemy I and was, unsurprisingly, dedicated to the Greek Muses. Queen Cleopatra VII, supposedly a scholar of some ability herself, would have been familiar with the Museum of Alexandria and its association with the Muses – indeed, the queen herself was named after the Muse Clio.

However, as we know from the recent history of the Taliban of Afghanistan, if the fundamentalist theists take control of society, then all of these areas of study and enjoyment are instantly banned – for god does not want his wisdom challenged by mere mortals (or rather the fundamentalist theists do not want independent, freethinkers punching great holes in their unsubstantiated arguments and their illogical assumptions).

This was likely to have been the fate that Mary Magdalene was suffering at the hands of the misogynist Saul. Mary was not a 'sinner', as the New Testament scribes try to impress upon us, she was an educated and liberated woman in the Egyptian and Parthian royal tradition. Music, song, poetry and dancing were encouraged in the Egyptian, Persian and Parthian royal courts, and no doubt Mary was proficient at all these arts, and probably many of the sciences too. The fact that this is true is made perfectly clear in the Gnostic gospels from the Nag Hammadi collection. Here, it is made perfectly plain that Mary was a senior disciple of Jesus, perhaps even his 'right-hand man' *(sic)*, as the *Last Supper* painting by Leonado da Vinci strongly suggests. In the Gospel of Mary it is said:

> Then Mary stood up ... and said to her brethren, 'Do not weep and do not grieve ... for his grace will be entirely with you and will protect you.' When Mary said this, she turned their hearts to the good and they began to discuss the words of the saviour.
>
> Peter said to Mary, 'Sister, we know that the Saviour loved you more than the rest of women. Tell us the words of the Saviour which you remember – which you know but we do not, nor have we heard them.' Mary answered and said, 'What is hidden from you I will discuss with you.' And she began to speak to them. [N34]

Firstly, it should be noted that Mary greets the disciples as 'her brethren', and while this may be an allusion to the members of a congregation or Church, many of the disciples may well have been Mary's real brothers. In the book *Jesus* I made a strong case that Mary was both Jesus' wife and his sister, and that their incestuous union was derived from the traditions of the Egyptian royalty. The evidence presented in this book can only serve to confirm this assertion, for we know that Thea Muse and Phraataces indulged in a similar incestual union. Were Jesus and Mary to be descended from this Egypto-Parthian royal line, their sibling marriage is not only likely, it is almost a certainty.

Secondly, it can be clearly seen from these two short paragraphs that Mary Magdalene was not only well versed in the secrets of the Church of Jesus and James, but that she was perhaps also its highest initiate. Certainly she was well above Peter, who went on with Saul-Josephus to found the rival Catholic Church, and so Mary must have been fully 'inspired' with knowledge and gnosis. But this deep knowledge caused friction within the uninitiated disciples:

> But Andrew answered and said to the brethren, "Say what you wish about what she has said. I at least do not believe that the saviour said this. For certainly these teachings are strange ideas." Peter answered and spoke concerning these same things. He questioned them about the saviour: "Did

> he really speak with a woman without our knowledge and not openly? Are we to turn about and all listen to her? Did he prefer her to us?" Levi answered and said to (Simon) Peter, "Peter, you have always been hot-tempered. Now I see you contending against (Mary) like our adversaries. But surely if the saviour made her worthy, who are you to reject her? Surely the saviour knows her very well. That is why he loved her more than us." [N35]

Note that Simon Peter is being called 'hot-tempered', for this is exactly what his name means in the Egyptian, as has already been explained in an earlier chapter. It is also clear that Mary's deep gnosis and understanding was causing friction within the early Church, and no doubt when the Church of Saul split from the Church of Jesus and James, the education of women was one of the first things to suffer. So, in the eyes of the Christian Taliban, the position of female disciples and saviours was deemed to be desperately heretical, and so Mary Magdalene was denied her gnosis or knowledge. In other words, the seven Muses (the seven evil winds) were chased out of Mary Magdalene, and through this process she was 'healed' of her heretical knowledge (gnosis).

While I cannot say for certain that this is the absolute truth behind this particular verse, my reinterpretation does seem to make a great deal more sense than the original. However, if this is so, then it does mean that there is a tangible and compelling link between Mary Magdalene and the seven (or nine) Muses of Greek mythology. In other words, there is a compelling link between Mary Magdalene and Thea Muse Ourania, the queen of Parthia and Thea Muse Cleo-Patra VII, the queen of Egypt. The precise manner in which Mary was descended from Thea Muse will be discussed in the next chapter.

VII

Who's Who?

The evidence is clear. Mary and Joseph, the mother and father of Jesus and Mary Magdalene, must have been related in some manner to the exiled family of Thea Muse and Phraataces. But if this is the case, then who, exactly, was who?

The first and most obvious candidate for Mary, the mother of Jesus, was Thea Muse herself. However, biology would argue against this association, for to have been a daughter of Julius Caesar, Thea Muse must have been born in 44 BC. But Jesus was most probably born in AD 6, which would have made Thea Muse 50 years old at the time of his birth, and while this is not an entirely impossible age for a mother, it has to strongly count against her; especially if the brothers and sisters of Jesus were his younger siblings, as one might expect. The alternative, and more likely, candidate for Mary must therefore be the daughter of Thea Muse, who was called Julia Muse Ourania. Note again that Thea Muse's daughter used the nomen of the Julia family, which demonstrates that Thea Muse was the daughter of Julius Caesar; for why else would an Egypto-Parthian queen name her daughter after a Roman emperor?

The date of birth for Julia Ourania is uncertain, but perhaps we can confidently predict that she would have been born shortly after Thea Muse's marriage to Phraates IV. The best guess for their marriage is 25 BC, and so we could place the birth of Julia Ourania with some confidence to about 20 BC. This would make Julia Ourania, the biblical 'Virgin' Mary, 26 years old at the time of Jesus' birth (presuming that the Roman taxation of Judaea under Cyrenius represents the true date for the birth of Jesus). So although the biblical name may appear to be 'incorrect', this birth date would certainly suit the daughter of Thea Muse very well.

The reason for the biblical accounts using a different name has already been covered. Firstly, it was not in the interests of either Saul-Josephus or the resulting Christian administration to reveal that their Messiah was born of an Egypto-Parthian princess, for that went against every aspect of the disinformation that they were trying to peddle to the faithful. By necessity, an alternative name had to be used. Secondly, it has already been explained that Mary is not a name but a title, meaning 'Love (Goddess)'. This simply identified Mary as a God's Wife, the high priestess of the temple who attended to the sexual needs of the gods and who was possibly an incarnation of Isis too. Thus, the change from Julia to Mary was not a lie, as such; instead it was a deliberate deception, in order that the links with Egypt and Parthia could be broken.

However, the tradition that Mary was somehow linked to a Parthian queen called Thea Muse must have been very strong in the centuries after Jesus' death, for the Renaissance artists drew upon these ancient traditions and depicted Mary (the 'Virgin') in a consistent and particular manner. The typical imagery of Mary, the mother of Jesus, which evolved in ecclesiastical traditions, was of a young lady dressed in blue and white robes, standing upon the crescent Moon and having twelve stars arranged in a circle around her head. Two versions of this kind of depiction are shown in the colour section, and this imagery is taken from a verse in Revelations which says:

> And there appeared a great wonder in heaven; a woman clothed with the Sun, and the Moon under her feet, and upon her head a crown of twelve stars. [B1]

Although the Bible does not mention the colour of Mary's robes, the Mandaeans do. The goddess in question was called Ruha, and since she was known as the Mother of all Planets, we can confidently identify her with Isis, the Queen of Heaven, and thus with Muse Ourania (the Greek goddess) and finally with the biblical Mary herself. But the Mandaean texts go on to say that the colours of Ruha's robes were sky blue and pale cornflower, which is much the same as the colours adopted by later Western artists for the 'Virgin' Mary's robes.

The twelve stars that were arranged in a circle around Mary's head are perhaps representative of the twelve disciples or the twelve sons of Jacob. However, all of these biblical gatherings that come in dozens were fundamentally based upon the twelve signs of the zodiac, as Josephus makes plain in his accounts. This demonstrates the original astrological and astronomical foundations of Judaeo-Christianity, which have been successfully obscured and covered up in more recent times. Again, this is why Jews in the first centuries AD commissioned mosaics of the zodiac for the floors of their synagogues.

The twelve stars also demonstrate that Mary is again to be identified with Muse Ourania, the Greek goddess of astronomy who was known as the Heavenly Muse Ourania and who foretold the future by looking at the positions of the stars. In other words, Muse Ourania was the original Greek astrologer goddess. Note, however, that the later artistic interpretations of the Greek goddess Muse Ourania, with her blue and white cloak and a ring of stars around her head, are more or less identical to those of Mary the 'Virgin'. See the colour section for an example of this striking similarity. Clearly, Mary, the mother of Jesus, is being portrayed as an incarnation of the Greek goddess Muse Ourania; but why should this be so? Was Mary to be identified with the heavens? Was she being depicted as the Queen of Heaven, an incarnation of the Egyptian Isis? Or was she being portrayed as Thea Muse Ourania, the Queen of Parthia?

The Moon under the feet of Mary may supply us with another clue in this regard, for the Moon is an image of Selene, the Greek goddess of the Moon, the sister of Helios. But Cleopatra Selene, if readers will recall, was the daughter of Cleopatra VII who married Jubba II of Mauretania. Thus this image of Mary standing upon the Moon (Selene), yet crowned with twelve stars (Muse Ourania) can now be seen as an image of Thea Muse Ourania Selene, the first daughter of Cleopatra VII. Just as Cleopatra Selene, the second daughter of Cleopatra VII, was identified with the Moon, I have no doubt that Thea Muse of Parthia was identified likewise. So the image of Mary dressed as the Greek Muse Ourania, but simultaneously standing upon the crescent Moon of Selene, identifies the mother of Jesus with Thea Muse Ourania, the Queen of Parthia; the only caveat to this being that Mary would have to have been the daughter, Julia Muse Ourania, for Thea Muse Ourania would have been past childbearing age in AD 6.

This imagery of Mary is, of course, a very symbolic arrangement that has lasted though the ages and been absorbed into our modern national and political systems. The flag that was chosen to represent the unity of Europe, for instance, comprised a circle of twelve golden stars upon a blue background. For some time the pretence of the twelve stars representing twelve nations of the union was maintained; but as the EU grew ever larger the number of stars did not, and so the pretence quietly faded. In truth, it is highly likely that this EU imagery instead represents Mary, and the continuing bloodline of the biblical family in Europe. However, this symbolism may also be demonstrating a reverence for the cult of the Queen of Heaven that goes back to the veneration of the Queen of Sheba and to Isis herself.

VII *Who's Who?*

Joseph

The next character that we need to identify in the biblical record is Joseph, the father of Jesus. The first candidate for this position has to be the husband-son of Thea Muse, namely Prince (King) Phraatces. Thea Muse's son would have been born around the same time as Julia Ourania, say about 24 BC, which would make him about 30 years old at the time of the birth of Jesus. Although the Christian Church tends to assume that Joseph was much older than Mary, his wife, there is actually no evidence for this. The only thing we do know is that he disappears early in the story for some reason, perhaps because he died before the main events in Jesus' life occurred.

In the classical interpretation of Jesus' life, this would mean that Joseph died before AD 30, and Jesus' presumed crucifixion at this time. If, however, we assume that this date represented Jesus' third-degree initiation, and that Jesus was still active in Judaea during the run-up to the Jewish Civil War, as Saul-Josephus maintains, then Joseph need only to have died prior to AD 65. If the persecution of the Church of Jesus by Saul-Josephus occurred in about AD 65, then Jesus would have been 59 years old at this time and his mother a not so impossible 85.

We have no historical information whatsoever about the eventual fate of Prince (King) Phraatces, and so there is no way of knowing if he married his sister, Julia Ourania [Mary], or not. However, there is another possible spouse for Julia Ourania [Mary], and that is Ptolemy of Mauretania. If we recall the opening chapters of this book, it was stated there that Cleopatra VII's daughter by Mark Antony, Cleopatra Selene, was taken to Rome as a hostage. She was later betrothed to Augustus Caesar's close friend Jubba II of Mauretania, who was given the kingdoms of northern Africa to rule as a client king of Rome. Jubba II was a wise and reliable monarch who made these provinces relatively prosperous, and who in turn secured the southern borders of the Roman empire for Augustus. It is believed that Jubba and Cleopatra Selene had at least two children, a daughter named Drusilla and a son called Ptolemy. Note that it was Queen Cleopatra Selene who was considered the more illustrious of these two monarchs, for the son's name continued the Egyptian dynasty and not the Mauretanian royal line.

The history of this Mauretanian kingdom is sketchy to say the least, but there is a suggestion that Julia Muse Ourania of Syrio-Judaea married Ptolemy of Mauretania.

> (Ptolemy) probably married a queen (Julia) Ourania, known only through a funerary inscription of her freedwoman Julia Bodina at Cherchel. [2]

As dynastic alliances go, this union would actually make a great deal of sense. Julia Ourania was the granddaughter of Cleopatra VII of Egypt and Julius Caesar, with some intermingled royal Parthian blood as well. On the other hand, Ptolemy of Mauretania was the grandson of Cleopatra VII and Mark Antony. What a glorious mix of bloodlines this union would have fused together; and so this mere suggestion, which was derived from a funerary inscription of a servant in the royal court of Mauretania, just has to be a historical possibility. Such a royal alliance held up the possibility of uniting Rome, Egypt and Parthia under the banner of one illustrious royal family. It would have been an opportunity that was too good to miss.

In Chapter V it has already been demonstrated that Jesus was called Ben Pandera and thus his father, Joseph, was called Pandera or Pa-ndjer-Ra. But it was Caesarion Ptolemy of Egypt, and presumably also his nephew Ptolemy of Mauretania, who was also called Pandjer-Ra  in this era, while another of his titles can be read as meaning 'Saviour'. Thus the titles that the Talmud ascribes to Joseph closely match the titles of Ptolemy of Mauretania.

Had the biblical Joseph been Ptolemy of Mauretania, there would also have been a good reason for his disappearance from the biblical accounts. Ptolemy was king of Mauretania between 21-40 AD, initially in a co-regency with his father Jubba II. Upon the death of his father in AD 23, Ptolemy assumed full control of his kingdom. In AD 24 he fought and won several battles against marauding tribes in North Africa, which secured Rome's southern borders once more, and for which he was awarded the ivory sceptre. However, in AD 40 the emperor Caligula invited Ptolemy to Rome, and Ptolemy made the fatal mistake of wearing a purple cloak. No doubt Ptolemy wore the cloak because he regarded himself as the true successor of the empire of Mark Antony and Cleopatra VII, and so he was displaying himself as the true king of the Roman empire. Had his wife been Julia Muse Ourania, his self-confidence may have been considerably enhanced, as he would have been the founding father of a great new Egypto-Roman-Parthian dynasty. But, in this case, the perceived threat to Caligula's throne would have been proportionately increased.

If Ptolemy thought that the public adulation of Rome would increase his prestige, then he spectacularly miscalculated his status. The much more predictable result of wearing his royal cloak of purple was that, in a fit of rage, Caligula had Ptolemy of Mauretania executed. Thus, according to classical history, one of the last branches of the Ptolemaic dynasty of Egypt had been extinguished. So, if Ptolemy had been Joseph, he would not have been mentioned in any of the biblical accounts that followed the year AD 40, which is what we find. But, of course, if Joseph were a

Fig 37. Ptolemy of Mauretania.

pseudonym for Ptolemy, then the royal Ptolemaic line had not been extinguished at all, for Joseph had at least four sons and two daughters.

If this was the true ancestry of the biblical Joseph, then there is another reason for sidelining him from the biblical accounts; for in the guise of Ptolemy of Mauretania, he was the only member of the biblical family who was well known in this era and thus well known in the historical record. Thea Muse Ourania and Julia Muse Ourania had been exiled from their former homelands, and so in terms of Roman and Judaean politics and history they were virtually unknown. Ptolemy, however, was the son of a favourite of Augustus Caesar, and well known in the Roman political arena. Any mention of Ptolemy within the New Testament accounts would have destroyed the popular image of a poor 'carpenter', and so Joseph became a shadowy figure who was almost entirely deleted from this story. In addition, since Ptolemy and any of his potential offspring were obviously a direct threat to the rule of the emperors of Rome, it would not have been in Saul-Josephus' interest to advertise the fact that Ptolemy had a number of surviving sons who were creating a rebellion in Judaea. If Saul-Josephus' texts (the New Testament and *Jewish War*) were to survive in a Roman world, they had to separate the family of Jesus from the Egyptian Ptolemaic royal line.

Another point to make is the resulting status of Julia Ourania. If she had married Ptolemy she would have become Queen of Mauretania, and would have taken up residence in the court of Ptolemy in north Africa. But this presents us with a problem. For Jesus to have been born in Judaea (Bethanya or Aurania), it is more likely that Jesus was actually the son of Julia Ourania and Phraataces. Thea Muse and Phraataces were exiled to Bethanya or Aurania in 4 BC, and since Phraataces had already married his mother, it is not beyond the realms of possibility that he also married his sister. This would place the birth of Jesus in exactly the right location and at exactly the right time. In support of this argument, when talking about Philip of Gamala and the Babylonians of Bethanya, Josephus says:

> Now there was one Joseph, the son of a female physician, who excited a great many young men to join with them. He persuaded (the people of Gamala) to revolt from the king and take up arms. [J3]

However, the word being used for a physician is *magi*, the Magi kingmakers of Parthia. Who else could be the female Magi in this account, other than Thea Muse? The son of Thea Muse was, of course, Prince Phraataces, so this passage would suggest that Phraataces was Joseph, rather than Ptolemy of Mauretania. But the account is interesting nonetheless, as it places the name 'Joseph' in the right context and era.

However, the biblical accounts then insist that Mary [Julia Ourania] and Jesus fled to Egypt. It is said that this was to protect Jesus from King Herod the Great, who did not appreciate a pretender to the throne being born in his own back yard. This is possible, but the king in question at this time would have had to have been 'King' Herod Archelous, the tetrarch of Judaea, and not King Herod the Great. Thus the killing of the innocents, if it did happen in the manner that the New Testament claims, occurred in AD 6 and not 4 BC.

This would imply that Julia Ourania [Mary], the daughter of Thea Muse, fled to Egypt with her newborn son, who we can now call Jesus, in AD 6 or 7. The reason for travelling to Egypt was that, being the granddaughter of Cleopatra VII, Julia Muse Ourania ought to have been reasonably safe there; and her son could also be schooled in the ways of the Egyptian royalty and priesthood at the great temples of either Heliopolis or Alexandria. However, it is always possible that Mary [Julia Ourania] travelled a little further than Egypt and ended up in North Africa – in Mauretania perhaps. The intriguing possibility, once more, is that Julia Ourania became the wife of Ptolemy of Mauretania and not Phraataces.

The possibility also exists that Julia Ourania was married to Phraataces and then remarried to Ptolemy. While it might seem unlikely that a princess of Egypt and Parthia would be passed around from husband to husband in this fashion, this seems to have been a common event in this era. Felix, the procurator of Judaea in AD 54, boasted that he married three queens in succession, including Drusilla, the daughter of Ptolemy of Mauretania. Likewise, Princess Glaphrya of Cappadocia had three husbands, including Jubba II. Princesses appear to have been chattels of the state, to be married off and taken back from neighbouring monarchs and tetrarchs as and when the political situation demanded. Thus it would not have been unusual for Thea Muse to have spotted a dynastic alliance for her daughter, taken her away from her brother-husband, Phraataces, and given her to Ptolemy of Mauretania.

That there were close connections between Mauretania and Judaea is confirmed by Ptolemy's daughter ending up as the wife of Felix of Judaea. So how did this happen? Well, following the execution of Ptolemy at the hands of Caligula in AD 40, the kingdom of Mauretania was completely annexed by Rome. The royal court of Mauretania would, by necessity, have been forced into exile. Had Ptolemy been married to Julia Muse Ourania, as I strongly suspect, then the obvious place for their exile would have been back in Judaeo-Syria and the provinces of Bethanya and Aurania – especially if the latter had still been nominally autonomous from Rome. This is quite possibly how Drusilla, the daughter of Ptolemy of Mauretania [and Julia Muse Ourania], ended up marrying Felix of Judaea in about AD 40.

In other words, the Judaic prophecy was not quite fulfilled as intended. It may well have been that 'out of Egypt and North Africa I have called my son' – for Jesus and his siblings could have followed the same well-trodden path of exile and ended up back in Judaea in AD 40, just prior to the Jewish Civil War. Remember that my previous analysis of the New Testament, in the book *Jesus*, has already claimed that the majority of the New Testament events occurred in about AD 55 - 65, at the time when Saul-Josephus was the military commander of Galilee. Thus the date for the possible exile of Ptolemy's children back to Judaea ties in very nicely with what we know from the biblical accounts of the life of Jesus.

The prophet

Having discovered the true history of the New Testament family, perhaps we can now appreciate the reasons why so many theologians down the ages have sought to cover up the truth. What they sought to portray to the world was an icon of perfection; a role-model family who were supposed to have been related to some great spiritual entity who inhabited the Cosmos. What the diligent theological historians found, however, was a real conspiratorial royal family whose court intrigues shocked all and sundry, let alone the naive Christian priesthood. That these same theologians chose to alter the texts to suit the requirements of their propaganda should not come as a great surprise.

Having said that, it is quite possible that their conspiratorial obfuscation was completely unnecessary. The next prophet from this region was a self-confessed uneducated, self-centered, genocidal, racist and misogynist, whose favourite wife was only seven years old;* and yet the religion he founded is followed by hundreds of millions of people.

If one reads the verses from the Koran, it is blatantly obvious that Muhammad simply invented many of the pronouncements he supposedly received from god – the verses of the Koran – to suit his political, strategic and domestic requirements. Such was the ineptitude of the man that he even had to resort to inventing pronouncements from god to stop his various wives from fighting each other.** This was a man who could not even sort out his own domestic affairs, and yet he holds sway over the domestic living arrangements of all the Islamic world. Here is a man with an insatiable sexual appetite, who sanctioned the use of rape as a punishment, and yet he is taken to be a moral authority of a substantial proportion of the world's population. [4] It is not even as if we can consign this kind of abhorrent behaviour to the moral climate of the era in which Muhammad lived, for even his peers deemed his behaviour and morality to be deeply flawed. As the Edwardian historian Andre Servier said of these ancient commentaries:

> The problem with Muhammad's behaviour is not that he was a bedouin, but that he was a morally degenerate bedouin. [5]

The fact that millions of otherwise rational people will deceive themselves that this is not so, and that Muhammad was a virtuous role-model for society, demonstrates the depths of delusion that otherwise rational people will descend to in order to justify their chosen belief system. Rationality and logic are cast aside in the rush to follow a creed, no matter how

* Aisha, one of Muhammad's fifteen wives, was only seven and 'with the dolls' at the time of her marriage. Muhammad was 44 years her senior.

** The verse reads as:

> If you two (Hafsah and Aishah) turn to god in repentance you shall be pardoned; but if you conspire against him (Muhammad), know that god is his protector. ... It may well be that, if he divorces you, the lord will give him in your place better wives than yourselves. [6]

Ibin Warraq says of these and other similar verses:

> The conclusion forces itself upon us that in later life, (Muhammad) consciously fabricated 'revelations', often for his own convenience, to sort out his domestic problems. [7]

contradictory, antisocial or evil it may be. In the process, mankind ends up being governed by the moral equivalents of Sun Myung Moon and Ron Hubbard – the spiritual leaders of the Moonies and the Scientologists respectively. If religion were a democracy, then these degenerate individuals could be consigned to the history books after five years; but it is not, and only a popular uprising like the Renaissance, Lutherism or the Enlightenment can correct the gross errors of the past.

Another mystery of gargantuan proportions is why many within the general population warm to the pronouncements of the uneducated and illiterate. Even within Christianity they try to take an educated prince and turn him into an illiterate pauper, in order to make his pronouncements more acceptable to the faithful. In a similar fashion, Muhammad was unable to read or appreciate the great traditions of Persian and Parthian art, music and poetry; and when the intelligentsia mocked his rustic ignorance, Muhammad's 'god' (Muhammad himself) swiftly forbade the pleasures of the arts.

> Afak mocked Muhammad in verse, especially his desire to control people's lives ... (Muhammad) simply commented "who will deal with this rascal for me?" – and one of his 'weepers' did. That a poet of so advanced an age should be murdered for a verbal sleight would have been inconceivable under the previous Arab custom. [8]

The quote is reminiscent of a famous cry of exasperation from Shakespeare's Henry II, "Will no one rid me of this turbulent priest!". Obligingly, someone in Muhammad's army did just that, and there was no more mockery of the prophet's ignorance. But herein lies a great problem, for instead of humankind being governed by a meritocracy (leadership by the highly educated and most able), we end up with either a mediocracy (leadership by the average) or ignocracy (leadership by ill-educated fools). It is beyond understanding that we should allow the ignorance and envy of a seventh century AD individual to result in the Taliban of the modern era banning song and dance, but it happens nonetheless. Likewise, in modern Britain, we are similarly supporting the destruction of all the nation's best schools, in order to assuage the ignorance and envy of a politician who failed his senior school entrance examinations at the tender age of eleven. How little we have progressed over the centuries!

Perhaps the moral of this whole tale is that it is patently obvious that nations are governed by the whims and desires of men and women, and not by the dictates of any magnanimous spiritual entity. No self-respecting, all-powerful god, should such a thing exist, would play a partisan role in the disgraceful politics of mankind, and any such entity must be observing our world and shaking their head(s) in disbelief. Thus, the many calls for god to bless this or that nation are simply extensions of the age-old propaganda that has been preached from many a bloodstained pulpit over the millennia. That otherwise sane people all over the world should still believe that an unimaginably intelligent and powerful entity would stoop to such levels, and effectively sanction the murder of great swathes of his or her own creation, demonstrates how ignorant and devoid of understanding much of humankind still is. Seneca the Younger, the first century Roman philosopher, said of theology:

> Religion is regarded by the common people as true, by the wise as false, and by rulers as useful.

Were this ancient pearl of wisdom to be displayed above the entrance to every single church, synagogue, mosque and temple across the globe, the world would undoubtedly be a better place.

True Testament

The evidence that has been outlined at length in this book is, in my opinion, the true history and ancestry of the New Testament family. As I had long suspected, the biblical family was indeed of royal blood, and in truth its members were descended from all three of the great empires of the ancient world: the Egyptian, the Roman and the Persian. Had this illustrious family found a vacant throne and seized their opportunity, they would probably have been the most powerful of all the royal lines to rule in the first century AD. But it was not to be.

Josephus records that there was a military foray into Parthia around AD 36, led by another Prince Tiridates, who is said to have been a grandson of Phraates IV. Had Jesus been the son of Julia Ourania, he would indeed have been Phraates' grandson. This Roman-backed incursion into Parthia was obviously instigated by the Parthian (Babylonian) exiles in Gamala [Jimal], and so this military adventure is likely to have involved the biblical Jesus (but Jesus' use of the Roman military as allies must have angered the Parthians and Jews in equal measure). With the backing of several Parthian nobles, Seleucia surrendered and Tiridates III [Jesus] was crowned as king of Parthia. But the presence of Romans in the country angered many Parthians, and so King Artabanus II was able to raise a large army and chase Tiridates III [Jesus] back to Syria. Thus [Jesus'] attempt to re-establish his royal line on a vacant throne was dashed. Likewise, Jesus' desperate attempt to take Jerusalem – both by guile and by force – was also thwarted.

VII *Who's Who?*

Following the Roman destruction of Judaeo-Israel in AD 70, those who remained of the royal New Testament family were scattered across the Mediterranean, where their descendants would intermittently gain and lose influence and power among the great royal houses of Europe. However, courtesy of the evangelical Saul-Josephus (Flavius), the biblical family's name and a record of their many deeds would spread around the world like a virulent virus. Yet despite this apparent success, the true regal nature of the New Testament family and their precise history and ancestry would be studiously deleted from each and every historical record. Perhaps we should remind ourselves why was this done.

Christianity was the Church of Saul-Josephus, rather than the Church of Jesus and James. It was Saul who took the life history of Jesus and mixed this with some of the basic theology of the Church of Jesus [the fourth sect], and formed a new religion that could be practised by Jews and Gentiles alike. But the new religion of Saul was often at odds with the life and beliefs of its primary icon, Jesus, and so the true ancestry of Jesus had to be glossed over. All Saul-Josephus wanted was an icon for people to worship, not a bloodline that could threaten his own position as Church leader. In a similar fashion, the new bishops of Rome, the Popes, assumed their great power by being the leaders of the Christian Church. The presence of a bloodline directly descended from Jesus could only threaten their position as pseudo-kings of the Church and diminish their massive secular and spiritual power – and so the Catholic Church and the bloodline descendants of Jesus have been at odds with each other ever since.

However, the ancestry uncovered in this book provides us with another reason for the sidelining of the family of Jesus. One of the great assets of Christianity, as it spread around the world, was that Saul-Josephus wove a great morality tale into his narrative. Thus the life and family of Jesus reads as an idyllic fantasy of love, sacrifice and the struggle against adversity and oppression. Mary and Joseph were being portrayed as the Waltons of the first century AD. But if the truth were known, the reality of Jesus' life was very different indeed. In fact, Jesus' grandmother, Thea Muse Ourania, murdered her husband, King Phraates IV. She then embarked upon an incestuous relationship by marrying her own son, Phraataces; a prince of Parthia who eventually became either Jesus' father or his uncle. The couple were then deposed and thrown out of their kingdom by the indignant aristocracy of Parthia, who frowned upon these ancient Egyptian customs of patricide and incest. The royal family were then forced to live in exile in Syrio-Judaea, from where they made efforts to attack Parthia and retake the throne in about AD 36. With this invasion being repulsed, they then planned to take Jerusalem by force, but yet again the efforts were all in vain.

This was the major reason for Saul-Josephus deleting the true ancestry and life of the biblical Jesus. The lack of information regarding Jesus' family was not due to his being totally unknown – it was because the true life of this royal family fell way below the ideals that Saul-Josephus wanted to preach from his pulpits. By all means and all devices, the truth about the court intrigues within this Egypto-Parthian royal family had to be excised from the history of Judaea and from the New Testament accounts. And, of course, it was Saul-Josephus who was in a unique position to actually achieve this, for as the founder of Christianity and the era's foremost historian he controlled the vast majority of the theological and secular history of the region.

It was Josephus, in the guise of Saul, who edited and published the religious history of Joseph and Mary and their family (the New Testament). Likewise, it was Josephus who wrote the secular history of Judaea *(Antiquities* and the *Jewish War)*. Thus Saul-Josephus was able to delete all the references from Judaic history that might have suggested that Mary was Julia Ourania, the daughter of Queen Thea Muse Ourania of Parthia.

Intriguingly, it should also be noted that Josephus was the only historian who wrote anything whatsoever about Thea Muse, which confirms that he did know of this history and wanted us to know something about it. His 'unreliable' testimony was vigorously denied by modern historians and only the later numismatic (coin) evidence from Parthia demonstrated that Josephus had, as ever, his finger on the pulse of Middle Eastern history. Saul-Josephus' reasoning for including Thea Muse in his (secular) history was probably twofold. Firstly, there was probably a little academic pride in that he knew a slice of history that few others did. Secondly, he may have deliberately made this inclusion in an attempt to make a clear differentiation between Thea Muse and the biblical Mary (for he had no idea what other historians in this era would write). His attempts at concealment eventually failed, but he did succeed in covering up the true ancestry of Jesus and Mary Magdalene for over two thousand years.

Having rediscovered the true ancestry of Jesus, after two millennia of obfuscation, the intervening centuries have bequeathed a long and convoluted footnote to this family history. It would seem that Jesus, as a son of Julia Ourania, failed in his first century AD attempt to re-establish his Egypto-Parthian royal family at the vanguard of a unified Romo-Parthian empire. However, through the egocentric and vainglorious, but dogged and diligent, industry of Saul-Josephus, the family of Jesus did eventually conquer all of the Roman Empire and much of the Parthian Empire too. Thus, Jesus' campaign was ultimately successful and he did indeed sit upon the throne of Rome as a god incarnate, just as previous Roman emperors had done. But this conquest was an empty victory, for it was in name only. Despite Jesus' nominative success and world domination over two millennia, the ultimate question remains unanswered – could we yet discover a real family behind the victorious icon?

✠✠✠ End ✠✠✠

Appendix

AI

Genealogy of the Biblical Family

The following pages contain a genealogy of the biblical family, which has been linked into the known history of Rome, Egypt and Parthia. Readers may note one or two differences to the family histories that are given in the various text books and web pages that cover this era. However, having looked very carefully at some of these interpretations, it is apparent that some authors are not always taking biology fully into account, with unlikely or unfeasible births and marriages sometimes taking place. Some of these problems stem from the accounts of Josephus Flavius, which contain internal contradictions that may prove impossible to sort out and to square with other historical accounts.

Cleopatra of Jerusalem is a case in point, for she has a separate mention in Josephus, but her offspring appear to equate quite well with those of Miriame II, another wife of Herod the Great. I still think that these two ladies are the same individual, but other authors try to separate them and in the process develop other genealogical inconsistences. Inevitably, these genealogies come down to a personal preference and a best guess, and the following represents my attempt at this.

AI Genealogy

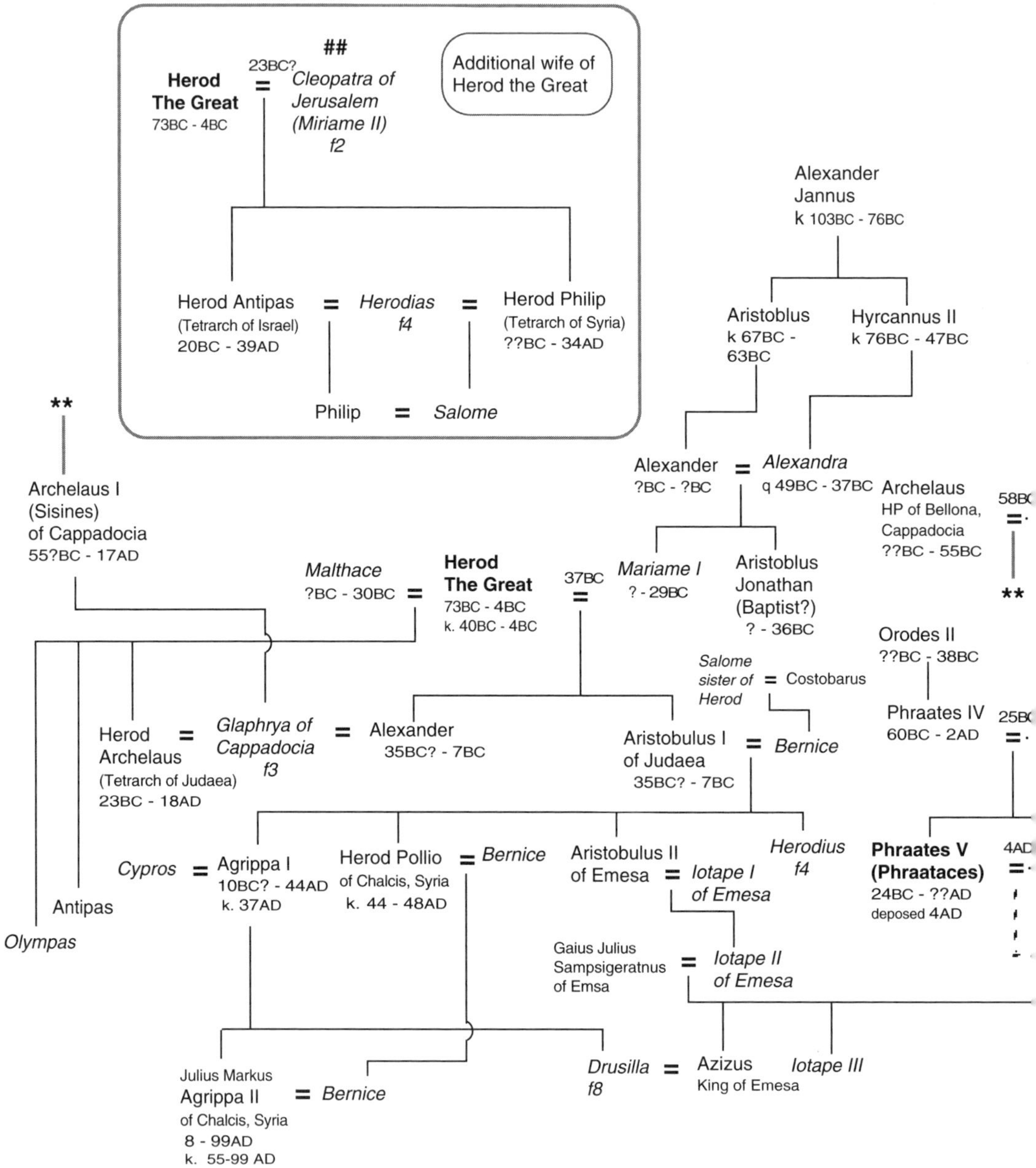

AI Genealogy

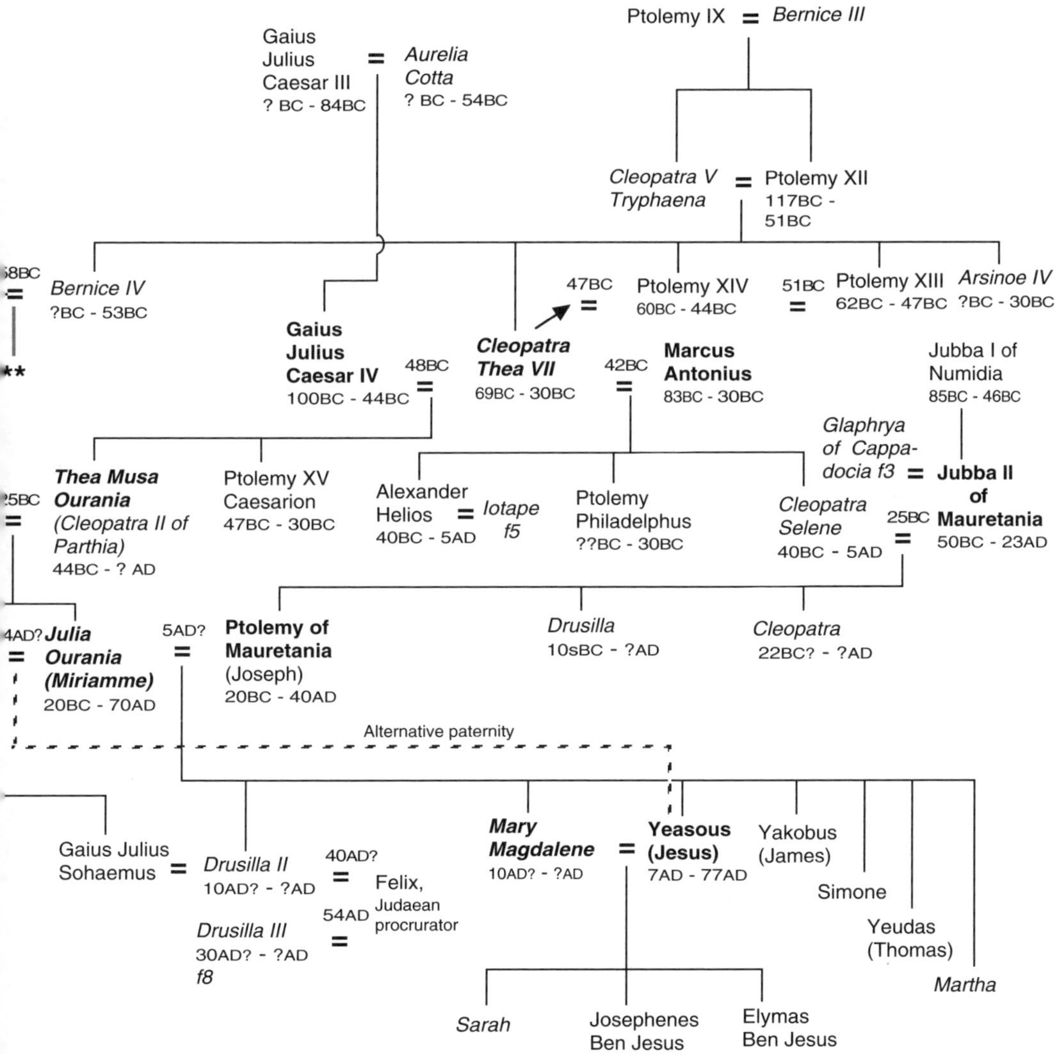

List of diagrams

Photo credits

Plate 1. The Death of Cleopatra, Jean-Andre Rixens.
Plate 2. Adoration of the Magi, Pieter Aertsen.
Plate 3. The Virgin Mary, Gornji Grad Cathedral, Slovenia. Ralph Ellis.
Plate 4. Virgin Mary depicted as Muse Ourania.
Plate 5. Muse Ourania and Calliope. Simon Vouet, Samuel Kress Collection.
Plate 6. The Beth Alpha zodiac, Israel.
Plate 7. The Sultan Tekesh mausoleum in Kunya Urgench.
Plate 8. The mausoleum of Jubba II and Cleopatra Selene, in Kolea, Algeria.
Plate 9. The ruined city of Umm el-Jimal in Aurania (Hauran). Ralph Ellis.
Plate 10-12.
Augustus Caesar, Julius Caesar, Vespasian. British Museum. Ralph Ellis.
Plate 13-15.
Cleopatra VII, Cleopatra VII, Thea Muse. British Museum. Ralph Ellis.
Plate 16-17.
Two coins of King Phraataces and Queen Thea Muse Ourania.

Notes & References

Bible: All references taken from the King James edition, although the text is often modernised for clarity.

Josephus: AA = Against Apion, Ant = Antiquities, JW = Jewish war, L = Life.
Page references are to the Loeb Classical Library system.
Quotes taken from William Whiston's translation, which was first published in 1736; some references are from the Penguin Classics edition by G. Williamson, first published 1959.

Manetho All page numbers are taken from the LCL edition, editor G. Goold.

Within the referencing system in this book, some of the reference numbers are prefixed with letters. This is to give the reader an idea of the source of the reference, without having to look up that particular reference. This only applies to the more popular reference works, and the following have been prefixed:

B = Bible, M = Manetho, J = Josephus, H = Herodotus,
T = Talmud, KN = Kebra Nagast, K = Koran, S = Strabo.

All references to Egyptian words are taken from:

An Egyptian Hieroglyphic Dictionary, E A Wallis Budge, Dover Publications. The entries in the dictionary are substantially in alphabetical (glyph) order, and so the references are easy to find and have not been listed in the references by their page number.

Notes & References

Chapter I

1. Josephus JW 1:364.
2. Bible 2 Peter 1:16.
3. The history of the early Church, H Lietzmann, vol 3.
4. Bible Re 19:7-9.
5. Ibid Re 21:9.
6. Babylonian Talmud Sanhedrin 106a.
7. Anthony and Cleopatra, W Shakespeare 2:2:200.
8. Plutarch, Caesar 49.
9. Catholic Encyclopaedia. http://www.newadvent.org/cathen/11712a.htm

Chapter II

1. Tombeua de la Chretienne, Marcel Christofle.
2. Josephus Ant 18:39.
3. Josephus Ant 2:47.
4. Hellenistic Queens, Prof Grace Macurdy p189.
5. Myth, History and Culture in Republican Rome; Cleopatra in Rome, by Erich Gruen.
6. Cicero, ad Atticum, 14:20:2, 14:20:2, 15:1:5, 15:4:4.
7. J. P. V. D. Balsdon, *Historia* 7 (1958) 80, 86 n. 37.
8. Hellenistic Queens, Prof Grace Macurdy p191.
9. Chris Bennett, Tyndale House, Cambridge UK. Residential Centre for Biblical Studies.
12. Chris Bennett, Tyndale House, Cambridge UK. Residential Centre for Biblical Studies.
13. Hellenistic Queens, G. H. Macurdy p190.
14. Hellenistic Queens, G. H. Macurdy p191.
15. Cambridge History of Iran, Vol 3a.
16. Metamorphoses or The Golden Ass Lucius Apuleius, Book 11, Chap 47.
17. Josephus Ant 2:232.
18. http://www.thekeep.org/~kunoichi/kunoichi/themestream/
19. C. Settipani, Continuit gentilice et continuit familiale dans les familles natoriales romaines: mythe et realit 438f n. 11.

Chapter III

1. Josephus Ant 4:63.
2. Augustus und seine Zeit, V Gardthausen.
3. Monumentum Ancyranum (Res Gestae Divi Augusti) See either the Loeb Classical Library or the web site on: http://penelope.uchicago.edu/Thayer/E/Roman/Texts/Augustus/Res_Gestae/5*.html
4. Josephus Ant 18:41.
5. Florus bkIV.
6. Strabo bk16:28.

7. Strabo, Geography bk 16:28.
8. Monumentum Ancyranum (Res Gestae Divi Augusti).
See either the Loeb Classical Library or the web address previously given.
9. Josephus Ant 18:39-42.
12. Monumentum Ancyranum (Res Gestae Divi Augusti).
13. The Cambridge History of Iran bk3a.
14. Josephus Ant 17:24.
15. Bible Jer 44:17.
16. Strabo Geography bk16, 2-34.
17. A commentary of the New Testament, John Lightfoot.
18. Dr. De Vries, professor of history at Calvin College in Grand Rapids, Michigan.
http://www.calvin.edu/academic/ archaeology/uj/publicat/interp/gem.htm
19. Ibid.
22. Ibid.
23. Ibid.
24. Ibid.
25. Ibid.
26. Ibid.
27. Ibid

Chapter IV

1. Bible Lu 2:1-6.
2. Josephus Ant 18:4.
3. Bible Acts 5:34-36.
4. Bible Mk 14:3.
5. Bible Joh 1:28.
6. The Mandaeans of Iraq and Iran, E S Drower bk 1.
7. The Mandaeans of Iraq and Iran, E S Drower bk 1.
8. http://www.israel-mfa.gov.il/MFA/History/Early%20History%20-%20
Archaeology/Archaeological%20Sites%20in%20Israel%20-%20
Gamala-%20Jewish%20Ci
9. Josephus Life 184.
12. Josephus Ant 18:9.
13. Bible Math 22:15-18, 21.
14. Bible John 2:15.
15. Josephus Ant 18:23.
16. Bible Math 4:10.
17. Josephus War 6:300.
18. Josephus Ant 18:6.
19. Bible Math 10:34.
22. Bible Lu 22:36.
23. Bible Lu 22:39-52. John 18:1-11. Math 26:47-55.
24. The original Greek text says Lestes ληστης, the primary Greek term for a Zealot.
The disciple called Simon was known as Simon Zelotes, or Simon the Zealot.
25. Josephus JW 261.
26. Bible Acts 21:38.
27. Bible Mark 6:31-44.

28. James, the Brother of Jesus, R Eisenman pxxvi.
29. James, the Brother of Jesus, R Eisenman pxxvii.
30. Bible Math 2:15.
32. Bible Math 13:55.
33. Josephus Ant 20:100-103.
34. Josephus L 66, 193, 200.
35. Josephus Ant 17:31.
36. Bible Math 9:10.
37. Commentary on the Bible, Adam Clarke 1832.
38. Bible Lu 2:7.
39. Bible Math 2:1-2.
42. Kebra Negast 30.
43. The Mandaeans of Iraq and Iran, E S Drower bk 1.
44. Bible Mt 2:16.
45. The Third Intermediate Period in Egypt, K Kitchen para 225.
46. Catholic Encyclopaedia.
47. Bible Math 2:13-15.

Chapter V

1. Geography, Strabo bk 16 2:34
2. James the Brother of Jesus, R Eisenman p847.
3. Catholic Encyclopaedia http://www.newadvent.org/cathen/15464a.htm
4. Shabbath 104 b.
5. Woman with the Alabaster Jar, Margaret Starbird.
6. Stranger in the Valley of the Kings, A Osman.

Chapter VI

1. Josephus Ant 18:23.
2. Bible Math 6:5-6.
3. Bible Mk 15:2.
4. Bible Mk 15:9-12.
5. Prophesies of Neferti, Ancient Egyptian Literature, M Lichtheim.
6. Bible 1Tim 2:9.
7. Bible 1Tim 2:12.
8. Tosephta Sanhedrin VIII, 7.
9. Koran 4:157. Many English translations will say 'it only seemed to them' or 'but they thought they did'. However, Prof Dawood, the translator of the Penguin Classics edition, says that the literal translation is 'he was made to resemble another for them'.
10. Recognitions, St Clement, I, 45 p497.
12. Dr. Lester Ness, PhD Foreign Affairs Dept, Changchun University, PR China.
13. Ibid. Extracts from: Sanctuaire Vincent p168; Naaran, Avi-Yonah p893; Symbols, Goodenough VIII.2, p168; Palestine Sukenik p29-30.
14. Bible 1Ki 15:12.
15. Bible 2Ki 23:7.

16. Shabbath 104b.
17. Bible Math 11:11.
18. Simon Magus: An essay 1892, G Mead pp28ff.
19. Bible Math 13:31-32.
22. Bible Math 13:33-34.
23. Bible Math 5:3, 10.
24. 'The New Colossus', a sonnet by Emma Lazarus pinned to the base of the Statue of Liberty.
25. Bible Math 10:7.
26. Bible Math 25:14-30.
27. Bible Math 18:1-4.
28. Bible Math 19:12.
29. Bible Math 22:1-10.
30. Josephus Ant 18:42.
32. Theos θεος refers to a masculine god, while Thea θεα refers to a goddess.
33. Bible Lu 8:2.
34. Gospel of Mary, Nag Hammadi Library in English, James Robinson.
35. Gospel of Mary, Nag Hammadi Library in English, James Robinson.

Chapter VII

1. Bible Rev 12:1
2. Prof Chris Bennett http://www.geocities.com/christopherjbennett/
3. Josephus Life 185.
4. The Sword of the Prophet, Serge Trifovic.
5. Islam and the Psychology of the Musulman, Andre Servier p20.
6. Koran 66:4.
7. Life of Muhummad, Ibn Ishaq. Quoted from The Sword of the Prophet, Serge Trifovic.
8. Life of Muhummad, Ibn Ishaq. Quoted from The Sword of the Prophet, Serge Trifovic.

Index

Index